A BOOMER CHICK'S GUIDE TO ONLINE DATING

Boomer Chicks rock!
Live everyday to the
fullest!

♡

Angela

A BOOMER CHICK'S GUIDE TO ONLINE DATING

You're Never Too Old to Look and Love

ANGELA I. SCHUTZ

A Boomer Chick's Guide To Online Dating Copyright © 2021 Angela I. Schutz

Paperback ISBN-13: 978-0-933578-04-3
E-book ISBN-13: 978-0-933578-05-0

Book design: Eddie Vincent
Cover photographs © Shutterstock

Published by Open Sesame Productions
Winchester, MA 01890
www.wii.fm

CONTENTS

DEDICATION

I dedicate this book to my family, who, although they never knew me, loved me unconditionally. To my granddaughter, please love yourself and never, never let anyone hurt you or put you down. You are perfect just the way you are. I will love you forever!

I also dedicate this book to Debra Poneman and my family from "Yes to Success." You have no idea how much your encouragement and acceptance has meant to me. We have each thrown the pebble across the vast ocean of life, and now we can reap the rewards as the ripples spread to make the world a better place in which to live.

I would be remiss if I didn't mention all of my truly loving friends, some of whom have been with me for more than fifty years. I am blessed by your presence in my life.

And to all the men I've known and loved: you were my inspirations and in some cases my muses. I have laughed with you and honored who you are. I have struggled to understand your perspective, but through it all, you have taught me so much. I love the male perspective, at least the part of it that I understand. We are so different, and despite the differences, we have found ways to love each other and learn from and inspire each other. I don't think it gets any better than that!

This book is purely meant to entertain, so Mr. Longface or the Italian Stallion should merely laugh at my rendition of our encounters. I am a writer. I love to tell a story. The facts are not facts, but merely my ponderings of what might have been. I do not mean to offend in any way. Enjoy the read. Have a laugh. Learn a lesson. With any luck you will have an aha moment that enlightens you as to why you did things in the way you did.

Honor yourself and be exactly who you were meant to be. The most beautiful person in the world is one who has stepped into her own skin and loves the woman she is. She radiates confidence…and that is sexy!

As women we are taught that we are not enough, not smart enough, not thin enough, you know the rest. Don't pay any attention to that. Spend time getting to know yourself. Know where your skills lie and cultivate them. Listen to your heart and be the best version of yourself you can be. Don't try to be like others…you weren't meant to be them, so don't try. I can't stress enough how important it is to be yourself.

And to you, the reader, thank you for reading my book. I hope it gives you some insight and some laughs because we all need that. I am grateful to share the planet with you and promise to do my part to leave this world better than when I joined it. I am excited for you and the journey you are on. Forge ahead, Boomer Chick; the best is yet to come.

PREFACE

"Every woman that finally figured out her worth, has picked up her suitcases of pride and boarded a flight to freedom, which landed in the valley of change."

- Shannon L. Alder

I know! Online dating past the age of 50 is beyond frightening, but this Boomer Chick can tell you it can create a sense of excitement and independence! I set some rules for myself: I would have no expectations that a knight in shining armor would ride in and carry me away, and I am "good enough"! I would make no apologies for any self-perceived imperfections. Any man who couldn't befriend me in my "as is" condition was not the man for me.

And so I jumped into the waters of online dating, feet first, eyes wide open, with a balance of scared anticipation and pure excitement. Once the journey began, I realized that I should share the lessons and insights I gained with other women in the hope that they would learn from my mistakes and my victories. I learned so much about my values and my desires. My passion for life grew stronger. I began to realize how important some things are to me, and I am actually not willing to give up on the things I truly value. I have also learned that a man with values, even those very different from my own, may not be willing to give up on those values. It takes a lot to have a meeting of the minds, but when the right man comes along, everything will suddenly make sense.

My best advice is: Don't settle! Take some time to develop the person you are and look for a man who will honor that. Find a reciprocal relationship with no stereotypical roles…each of you should do what you do best. Life is too precious to waste on vying for power. No one needs that. As a Boomer Chick, aim at a relationship that is filled with ease, love and mutual respect. Always strive to keep a sense of wonder at all the new things a relationship can bring. Throw fear out the window and enjoy the experiences. The bad experiences are simply lessons to be learned, and the good experiences are worth waiting for. Enjoy it all because you are worth it!

DATING DURING THE CORONAVIRUS

W ell, as of this writing, it's 2021, and we have all been challenged by the worst pandemic of our lifetime. Our entire country is struggling with trying to find a way to control this devastating virus. For those of us who are currently alone, the fact that we have had to go into quarantine has been such a challenge. When we venture out, we are expected to wear a mask and stay six feet away from every other person we encounter. We are all trying to maintain our health, and yet, as boomers we are still hearing the ticking of our life's clock ringing in our ears.

We were on dating sites because we no longer wanted to be alone. We were dreaming of finding a partner with whom to make memories on this final phase of life. Finding someone online who is interesting and who might be a potential partner now has the added problem of how to meet him and maintain social distancing. Can we get to know that "masked man" without seeing any more than his eyes? Are we willing to merely dream of his touch, his kisses, his loving embrace?

The sane answer is YES! This period in which we need to do everything in our power to stay safe and healthy will pass. Be safe, but you can still meet someone new as long as you both agree to maintain the necessary precautions. You can start by having Zoom meetings or talk on FaceTime so that you can actually see each other and get a sense of each other's personalities. Once you are comfortable, you can certainly make a date to go for a bike ride or a long walk where you can talk and get better acquainted.

As the bans begin to lift, you will be able to go out to dinner. If the weather is warm, choose a restaurant where you can eat outside on a patio. The positive that will come from all of this is that by having to wait to be close physically, you can use the time to develop a strong emotional bond. Learn about all of those things that make him special. What does he love to do? What has he accomplished in his life that he is proud of? Find your common bonds. What are your shared interests?

Spend some time dreaming of the day where you can meet and travel together. What is his family history? There are so many wonderful things you can find out about him and vice versa. By the time it is safe to meet, you will already know if he is someone you really want to meet. Most of all, be creative and find ways to date in a socially distanced world. Make it work without resentment. Look for the good in all the negativity associated with the Coronavirus. Don't put up self-inflicted roadblocks. Keep your mind and your heart open so that love can enter into your life. In the long run, it will be worth it!

Chapter 1

THE WHOLE TRUTH

I know! Online dating past the age of 50 is beyond frightening, but this Boomer Chick can tell you it can create a sense of excitement and independence like no other! Nine months ago I was just like many others. I couldn't imagine writing to strange (and in some cases, I do mean strange) men for the purpose of going on a date. The goal may have been friendship, companionship, or even a long-time relationship, but whatever the goal, the process scared me to death.

I set two rules for myself. One: I would have no expectations that a knight in shining armor would ride in and carry me away. Two: I would make no apologies for any self-perceived imperfections because I am "good enough." Any man who couldn't befriend me in my "as is" condition was not the man for me.

I have gone on many dates. I have had lots of fun. I have received gifts of flowers, perfume, jewelry and even a watermelon, but the greatest gift of all is that I have had the opportunity to really get to know myself. Independence is comfortably stepping into my own skin and loving it. I am a fairly creative woman who has the propensity for doing things just because they came up. So one night, I started thinking about what was missing in my life and what I had not yet tried that would bring some new perspective into my awareness.

I had spent many, many years trapped in a loveless marriage, and whether it was from some religious sense or mother's guilt, there I stayed being the dutiful wife and staying faithful and celibate in the sham of a marriage. Now, don't get me wrong, I believe there is a gift in every adverse situation, and I have worked hard to find the gift in this one, and here is what I've come up with. Although I was not in love with the man I married and the marriage became nothing more than two roommates, and bad ones at that, I was given the societal protection and stamp of approval that one gets from simply being married. Since my "husband" didn't really care all that much about me, I could come and go wherever and whenever I pleased. Doesn't sound so bad, does it, but factored in was my Catholic upbringing, and there you have it, the recipe for disaster!

I didn't want to stay, but couldn't leave, and my own sense of morality and ethics wouldn't allow me to cheat on this man as long as we were legally married. Now, to be fair, I will cast no aspersions against this man. He was simply not the man for me. We were polar opposites, and the longer I knew him, the less I could tolerate our differences. I am reminded here of something that I once heard Marie Osmond say, "We marry based on the level of our self-worth." Oh how true that is! I had no self-worth and thus married a man for all the wrong reasons.

If I were to give some advice here, it would be to tell everyone to spend some time in self-development and learn to appreciate the uniqueness of who you are and how wonderful and valuable all your skills and talents are to the world. This should be done long before you even think of marrying anyone. Be a whole person long before you enter into a couple's union. And while we are talking about this, the old adage *"to thine own self be true"* rings loud and clear in my ears now that I have grown to care about myself.

Talk about being between a rock and a hard place, there I was. Oh yes, I forgot to factor in that I had lived my life as the "fat" girl and so to say that I had no self-esteem was to be generous! Now, don't get me wrong. I don't want to paint the wrong picture here. I was far from a shrinking violet. The tenacity that kept me in the marriage was hard at work for me in all other areas of my life. Luckily, I really loved being with people and so I put myself into clubs and organizations that brought me sheer joy and allowed me to give love, platonic of course, to all sorts of people.

I have an engaging personality and make friends easily. I learned the art of being a leader and put it to use in many community ventures. I gathered skills and began to grow as a woman and a leader in my community. On the outside, no one would have a clue that I was crying on the inside for the lack of adult male-female love that most healthy heterosexual people need. My outer-world self was happy, confident and radiant. My inner-world self was sad and sex-starved. And did I say SAD??? Every night, sleeping in bed next to a man that I worked so hard for, but for whom I felt no love and from whom I got no love, was tragic.

I was a real woman whose needs were never met, so I adapted. I learned to be open and generous with the love and friendship I gave others. I became very intuitive and could recognize needs in others and gravitated towards them. I put on my "Superwoman" cape and scaled heights of success that surprised even me. But that longing for my outer and inner worlds to join into a blissful sea of happiness never happened. I constantly told myself that everything was okay and that someday, somehow, this man and I would part ways and I would then be free to find a man who would love the new and improved me. He would honor me and respect me and love me as only a man can do. That notion, that dream, that hope of having the love of a lifetime carried me through.

I worked hard at becoming a "new and improved" woman. I also learned to give others all of the qualities I so longed for from a man. I grew tender and gentle, kind and loving, generous and strong. I grew more spiritual and centered, learning that my strength comes from a Higher Being. I gave myself the gift of growth to make up for the lack of growth in my marriage.

Since there was no partnership, an element I assumed was inherent in every marriage, I had very little commitment toward trying to make it work. For all intents and purposes, it did work on a certain level. We looked like a couple. I was the wife who cooked and cleaned and accompanied him to events. I worked and paid for everything. Isn't that what marriage is all about??? I have met far too many people who view the love of their spouse as similar to that of a brother or sister, but there is no longer any physical attraction. Many of us feel and stay trapped in that limbo between the outward guise of being married and the reality of no longer acting married. My marriage had gone way past its expiration date and it really stunk!

One day some of us wake up and realize that there is more out there, and we go on an expedition to find what we are missing. We sometimes get caught up in the thrill of the hunt but know that there is a price to pay because true freedom does not come cheap. We long to capture that moment of ecstasy where longing and belonging collide into rapture. We long to put reality aside, if even for a moment, to allow wholeness to enter in and physical love to have its moment free from guilt.

For me, the day I woke up was the day I realized that I did not want to die never having had sex again! It was such a cruel thought. On one hand, I was trapped in a loveless marriage and on the other hand, passion and vitality were still coursing through my veins. I am still looking for the right moment, and I know I have definitely overthought this! Maybe I needed time to put some perspective on it, or maybe I simply needed to turn the key and let the chassis warm up to the idea, but for whatever reason, I got to the point where I felt it was necessary to allow myself the chance to find love.

Chapter 2

ENLIGHTENMENT

Since this is my story, I will tell you one more fact about me. I was a bright, creative, happy, but slightly wild child, who at the ripe old age of eighteen dropped out of college, never to return again, or so I thought! I went to work, got married and had a child. One day, when my son was twelve years old, he looked at me and said, "Mom, I hope you get your college degree before I get mine!" I was forty years old and horrified that this child, the receiver of all my unconditional love, was disappointed that his mom did not have a college degree. Well, I couldn't have it be this way, so the very next day I signed up to take classes at our local community college.

Life is truly a journey, and each day when we open our eyes, we have no idea where the path will lead us. I learned to be open to this new journey that included getting a formal education. It was fascinating to be the "mom" figure in a class of mostly eighteen-year-olds. It was actually fun to be the link between the instructor and the students. There were funny incidents that happened beyond all of the girls asking me for dating advice.

One day, I broke from the tradition of mindlessly going to the same seat in the classroom, as is traditional for all students even when the professor doesn't assign seats. I walked to the other side of the room and sat near a young lady in class. When the class was over, she looked me in the eye and said, "Don't ever sit next to me again!" I was horrified! Had I forgotten my deodorant or forgotten to freshen my breath? I didn't think so. I asked her what was wrong. What she said will forever be etched in my brain, "When you sit next to me, the professor looks this way because he expects you to always answer the questions no one else will answer, and I don't want him to look at me." Ah, the delights of being the oldest person in the class, sometimes even older than the professor.

I worked hard, and in the first two years got my Associate's Degree. In the next two years, I got my Bachelor's Degree, and in the next three years, my Master's Degree. Seven years, but I did it, and I will be eternally grateful that I did. Having the education that I thought I neither wanted, nor needed, was the turning point in my life.

Chapter 3

SUCCUMBING TO THE ALLURE OF ONLINE DATING

I don't think it unusual for a woman my age to be reluctant to try online dating. Those of us born before 1960 were not pre-programmed for all the technology or mindset needed to take part in this "sport." We were raised to think that people meet other people face-to-face first; you know that "don't talk to strangers" mindset. I always felt that social skills could only be assessed when you meet someone and see for yourself how they comport themselves. The very concept of "meeting" someone online for the purpose of "dating" is so foreign to me. Coupled with the baggage of a failed marriage and all that entailed, it was just too much to grasp.

The other thing that helps bind me to conventional wisdom is that I am clearly addicted to two current television shows. One is called "Dexter" about a serial killer who kills serial killers; not for the faint-hearted, but a show that I love. My other favorite is "Criminal Minds," which highlights the FBI's Behavioral Analysis Unit. The entire show is about how the FBI can profile violent criminals. With all the violence that I witness on TV, there is no wonder why I think online dating is strange and maybe even dangerous.

My mind is so full of horrific ideas that feel very real to me even though not based on reality.

Ah, so now you might be wondering why on earth I decided to take on this project of entering into the world of online dating for 30 days. Well, people I know who do it are having fun, and some have even met great guys online. Besides, who am I to say that current standards are wrong? I have always been fairly progressive in my thinking, and even though these are uncharted waters for me, why not try something new?

Of course, typical of my "fly by the seat of your pants" style, I entered into the world of online dating with absolutely no preparation and little to no knowledge of how to get around and explore the web. One decision I made was to stick with only one site, and I plunked down the money for one month. Twenty-five dollars later, I had a new password and was in! I invite you to join me on my adventure, and, hopefully, my mistakes won't be yours, but my successes will be helpful to you should you put yourself on this journey.

This book is my account of a newbie to the online dating scene. It is being written day by day so as to capture the exact experiences as they happen. As I write this, my fingers are crossed that this will be an enlightening journey from which you and I will both learn. So here goes...

Chapter 4

A WOMAN'S TURN ON

It took me some time to sign on since I didn't really know what I wanted in my profile. I am a businesswoman and hoped that there might be some professional businessmen on the site. I did not want my profile to be too stilted toward business because I am also very much a kid at heart. I love to laugh and think that life should be fun. It is much too short to spend the rest of the time I have left being sad, lonely, and miserable. I already wasted too much time in those conditions while married. Why keep that going?

So who is the new, online me? How do I capture my nature, my essence, my drive without sounding fake? How do I retain my privacy and still reveal a bit about who I am? Who wants to go out with a workaholic who has known very little more than working non-stop?

Once I got into the negative scripts that most of us get into when we doubt ourselves, I went right into the body imperfections and how I let myself go while struggling to stay married. Now who would want me? I had forgotten, of course, about how giving I am and how I am a prolific writer and a wonderful friend and person who loves to empower others. I had forgotten about all the community service I had done. It went out of my head as I started to write my profile. After all, I had no idea whether I was even ready for this journey, but I am a great believer in putting a stake in the ground and following through, even when you get cold feet after the journey begins.

Just do it! After I wrote my profile and uploaded a photo (there was the Doubter again messing with my head about which photo to use!), I checked out the tabs at the top of the page. I jumped into the Chat Room…no one there from my state. I chose a different state, only to find that the people in that chat room were really into graphic representations of their body parts and using lots of profanity. Whoa, I'm outta there right away. I tried several other states and found that most of the chat rooms were all about sex and included young, very hot participants. Not my style at all, so I immediately decided that the Chat Rooms weren't for me.

Next, I looked at the "Who's online" tab. Because my profile says that I am interested in men, there were pages and pages of photos of men glaring at me. It was a study in testosterone for sure! There were the hunters, the boaters, the jocks, the pet lovers, the athletes and all this information just from their photos!

I then proceeded to read some of the profiles. This was painful on so many levels. Since I am a writer, the written word is very important to me. Don't get me wrong, a simple mistake or typo doesn't bother me at all, but the complete inability to communicate using the written word is a bit of a turn off. Yes, my dear gentlemen, English class was important! I am not a snob, but your profile and your photo are the first impression I have of you. What are you trying to say to me if you are kissing your dog and can't string words together to make a complete thought?

Right now I have turned off all the men who are reading this book, but if you want to attract an intelligent, stable woman, I encourage you to rethink what you are putting out there online. For many of you, all you want is to feel the touch of a woman again. I get that, but what turns on most women is what her brain tells her about you. Want to turn me on? Tell me about the good that you do in the world. Tell me about what you are proud of. Tell me you love your kids. Tell me who you are and use English, please. I am not looking for a beach bum, so don't tell me that, and honestly, not every woman who goes online wants you to jump her bones through an email!

What comes next if you lead with what you want to do to me, this online stranger? There are plenty of pornographic sites out there if that's what you are into. I am not like that. Okay, so now you are wondering why I even started on this journey when sex isn't the first thing on my mind. Pretty naïve, huh? Isn't sex the reason EVERYONE signs onto an online dating site? Well, through this journal of my experience, we will find out.

Day One brought some interesting discussions with a man who did not seem the least bit interested in a sex-first approach. We exchanged several emails, and since no spark was generated, we simply stopped talking. I went through the "Who's online" tab for a while and sent out a few flirts consisting of the statement, "I like your profile." A few people responded before I called it a day, but nothing exciting happened. Not liking this very much, I signed off, hoping that things would get better tomorrow.

Chapter 5

MANEUVERING ANGRY MEN

I woke up early and signed right on. It looks like there is a lot of activity this morning. Several of the men I had sent a flirt to responded, and it gave me the chance to send out some emails. Wow! What came back was so interesting. First, Mr. Florida started off telling me about himself. He asked some decent questions and told me a bit about what he did before he retired and where he lived; a family man, who seemed proud of his kids and grandkids. Then the flood gates opened wide with his questions about sex and whether I masturbated! When I told him that I had no intention of answering such a question, he replied that it's just human and wondered why I didn't want to talk about it. He then asked me to email him – I don't think so.

Next, I had a few exchanges with a very nice younger man. We both knew that we would never be dating each other but would probably have a few friend exchanges. He was honestly a nice man and I wished him well. Then I was noticed by a very handsome, professional man with whom I also had a nice exchange. It was refreshing to talk with someone who could possibly get me.

As the day progressed, I got many flirts and emails from a wide variety of men. I answered some and totally ignored others. Some of the memorable ones turned out to be very different from anything I expected. One guy in a baseball cap, on the surface, seemed down to earth. He sent me an email telling me that he didn't meet my qualifications since he wasn't a businessman and he was turned off by my saying that I like a man who has a "glass is half full" attitude. He seemed to be saying that I was looking for a professional man who was rich! I emailed him back to say that I wasn't referring to money at all, but to a person's attitude about life, to which he said that there was no reason to comment on a rhetorical comment!

And then there was the Italian Lover. This guy was so funny in his emails…a bit forward, but quick and bright. We emailed back and forth for a while and then decided to use the instant messaging service so that we could really chat. Well, it was so much fun. We kept each other laughing for hours. It was a great exchange of quick comments…and then, all of a sudden he turned. His entire attitude changed. He decided that he no longer wanted to talk with me and slammed the figurative door in my face.

I didn't know what hit me. I went to bed confused and wondering where all of this was going. Did I fall into a pit of very angry men? What had they been through in life that left them so angry and so quick to lash out? It is going to be a bumpy ride for sure! Maybe some sleep will help. We'll see what tomorrow brings.

Chapter 6

PROFILE REVELATIONS

Day Three. This should be interesting! After all of my confusion on Day Two, I can't wait to see what today brings. I decided to drop the Italian Lover a very quick email to see if things were better after some sleep. Oh no, I was completely wrong. He lashed out again and so I decided to write him off as a non-contender. If he is so volatile in an email, I can't imagine how violent he might be in person. I was especially intrigued when I told him I was writing this book. He said, "RU KIDDING? You know nothing about online dating, and you pompously think you can write a book about it!" I foolishly tried to explain that it was precisely because I didn't know anything about navigating the online dating waters that the book would be helpful to other women like me. He told me I was a complete phony. I thought it was an interesting perspective, but that did not dissuade me from continuing to write!

My inbox was full of emails from all sorts of guys. Some didn't look like men I would want to meet, and then there were the emails from the very, very religious men who were certain that God put us together and they would be happy to relocate to where I live! REALLY! In your first email?

Are you going to buy me a ring in your second email?

Now I sound very cynical, something I have never been, but what's going on? Either my profile picture and write-up need to be changed, or I am just going to have to learn that this particular online dating service isn't what I thought it would be. Maybe I didn't read the fine print that says only sex addicts, religious zealots, and very angry men need apply.

The day is still young, so I will be anxious to see what comes later. I put it to rest for quite a few hours and then signed in again. Wow, nine men "noticed" me. I chose to answer a few, and a few told me that their service was nearly over, so they asked if I would email them directly. Then I noticed something about myself that truly shocked me. I looked at the name of one of the men and stereotyped him. I was shocked. I have friends from all over the world and I love them. I never see color or race, but here I made an assumption that this man was of a different race, based on his name. I hated my reaction and so decided to contact him. I was completely blown away at how wonderful this man was and how handsome. We emailed back and forth for a while and then we got onto yahoo chat. We talked for hours and hours, comparing notes and discussing all sorts of things. It was a really great evening and the start of my change in attitude about online dating.

After signing off with Mr. Bronx, I jumped back online one more time to see that nine more men had sent me messages. I answered a few and discarded the rest. I worried that I was crushing them. Think about it; you are making a desperate attempt to find love in this impersonal, online format and no one responds! How sad is that? I vowed that no matter what I think, I will at least say "Hi" to each man that reaches out.

Does this mean I really don't get this online thing? It was interesting that Mr. Bronx was so smitten with me that he asked me to delete my profile from the singles site! Oh no, my true self was showing! I gave him three very specific reasons why I would not take the site down, and one of those reasons was simply that I am not comfortable with a man, a strange man at that, telling me to take it down! Wow! Am I that hardened? Is this really a case of not wanting to be ordered around, or is it about my excitement with seeing this project unfold? I can't wait for <u>Day Four</u>!

Chapter 7

THE REALITY OF YOUR AGE

Woke up late and instantly thought about the events of last night. Mr. Bronx turned out to have a wonderful way with words. After we chatted for hours and signed off, I found that he had written me a beautiful email: deep perspectives on life with just a hint of the "fast and furious" approach attached to online dating. It seems that the way in which he differs from most is that his "fast and furious" is centered more on the "let's live happily ever after" rather than the "fast and furious" approach of the other guys who are centered on the age-old question "when will we have sex?"

The virtual world is interesting in that some people get right in your online face and make it known that if you are online, you should only be interested in one thing: SEX. Some are simply lonely and wax nostalgic for the companionship of a woman. Often they are widowed and probably had a good marriage, or at least the memory of one. They seem to be less focused on the physical rewards of a relationship and more on the emotional well-being from having a partner with whom to share everything. They remember that feeling of wholeness that comes from being a part of something – part

17

of a family, part of a couple, part of a team or group. They remember how great it is to have someone in your life who is reciprocal and who can melt you with a look – either in a good way or bad!

The human condition seems to thrive on connections and relationships, yet so many have no idea how to handle a relationship when one is presented. Did Mr. Florida really think that by email #2 we would be talking about masturbation? Did the Italian Lover think I would sigh and call him "my man" by insulting my integrity and telling me I "had to grow a pair" because I didn't think sex was in fact the only thing that mattered? Did my baseball capped angry "friend" really need to tell me he didn't meet my qualifications because he wasn't a professional businessman?

As this journey unfolds, I am also acutely aware of my reactions to the photos men put online and how young those fifty-one-year-olds look, except for that one guy who says he is fifty-one, but clearly looks seventy-one! I am pretty young at heart, but sadly, this experience is a true reality check…young, yes, but only at heart. This is, if truth be told, a lesson in how harsh gravity has been to me! Those "sixty-somethings" are looking better and better to me every day. My hope is that age, wisdom, and diminished eyesight will leverage my chances of getting a date with one of them.

So, my advice is that if you want to stay in your delusional world that tells you how much younger than your years you look, do NOT enter the online dating world. It will burst your bubble, and we all know how much that can hurt!

Well, let's go online to see what <u>Day Four</u> will bring. We are starting off quietly. One pleasantry from Mr. Longface just wanting to chat: okay, I answered, we can chat online. Another email saying that Wolf is interested in my profile. Is he a wolf? He looks like a nice guy, laid back and calm. Can I really tell all that from a picture? You know, that "worth a thousand words "thing? Some people seem to exude an air of calmness, even through a photo.

I have gotten several responses to my photo where men are saying things like I am "elegant," "fun-loving,"" professional," and "reliable" …a truly good woman. Can we really "see" all these attributes in a photo? Can we truly assess anything beyond our perception of beauty, or the lack thereof, or do we assign attributes to a photo based on our needs? How do we take that into the real world? Do we assign attributes to another person based on our personal needs rather than on the reality of who they are? Did Italian Lover really turn on me or did I simply run from the truths he told? Many would say we bring into our lives that which we most need, but do not necessarily want.

I think I need to re-evaluate all of my reactions to photos and responses. This is going to be harder than I thought. I just wanted a perspective on online dating, not to re-evaluate who I am! Well, maybe that's just the point! As I have learned from Jack Canfield, "when the student is ready, the teacher shows up."

Wow! By 4:00 pm. <u>Day Four</u> has exploded into an unbelievable collection of emails from all sorts of men. Now, after only four days I have 132 email messages! I smile and blush at some that are very sweet and/or very racy. Mr. Wolf is truly the sweet guy I thought he would be. Raises dogs. Nice, but I don't think he's too interested in me. Exchanged a few emails, but since he asks no questions, it is very hard to keep going.

Mr. Stamp Collector is also a nice guy. I bet he is a wonderful grandpa. His emails are very down to earth. He is looking to make a connection with me. I bet he would be fun to spend some time with…good clean fun with absolutely no pressure. The kind of man that appreciates a woman and would treat her like a lady. The kind of guy you could have a cup of coffee with and talk for hours. Like him so far.

And there's Mr. 45! Wow, such a fun guy, but does he really have to be 45? UGH. I know better than to cross the age gap line. It could never be a pretty picture when a guy's friends compliment his mother and she's really his girlfriend. We played. We chatted. We played. We chatted. Then I did something I never thought I would do. I called him on the phone when he asked me to. Seems like crossing the line to me. He's 45 for goodness sakes! What is the lesson here? I have endless energy, the kind that 65-year-old men cannot keep up with. I have a very quick mind and love someone who can banter back and forth with me quickly and sharply. I have a big spirit and a loving heart, so where is that man my age who can satisfy all of that? Mr. 45 is going to be a problem because, not only do I love his ability to banter with me and keep up with my funny quips, I love the resonance of his voice. Really sexy. Okay, Mr. 45, you are going to be my ethical problem and it's only Day Four.

Mr. Los Angeles just jumped on and noticed me. I am beginning to think I need to send flowers to the person who took my picture when I was on a cruise. It has captured the free spirit that I am, and I look so happy. Lots of men have noticed. Maybe this book should be called the Bachelorette after the TV show where one woman is given 25 men to get to know so that she can find the man of her dreams. I am beginning to feel like that – not the kind of life I have been used to in the past. Maybe I can learn to become a dating coach after my thirty days are up.

This is really an interesting experiment, but it is certainly not for the fainthearted woman. You need to be able to take rejection on a massive level, you need to be able to be disgusted and rise above it, and you need to be able to filter out your real feelings from the false hopes that come from being wooed by the insincere.

So my dear female friends, maybe the Italian Lover was right when he told me I "needed to grow a pair." Oh, by the way, Mr. Bronx turned out to not be the stand-up guy he presented himself to be. He made me promise to be on Yahoo IM at 7:00 pm, but did he show up for his "soulmate"? Heck no! Here he wanted to relocate for me because God sent me to him. Where are you, Mr. Bronx? In the gutter with all of the other guys who don't have the maturity to say, "I'm sorry, I don't think this is going to work out?" Maybe they become those same guys who interview you for a job and never call you to tell you they've picked someone else. I am beginning to see why we are all so frustrated in this country.

And then, at the other side of the spectrum, is Mr. Pilot. Such a nice person to talk with! Probably someone who would be a good friend, but unlikely someone I would ever date. He is smart, writes well and knows that in order to keep a conversation going, you write and you ask a question so that the other person can answer. See Mr. Wolf, it's easy – just like waltzing: one, two, three, one two, three, one, two three.

Well, the night has shaped up in the most unusual way. Mr. 45 talked with me for such a long time. He started off as a wild flirt and ended up being a real mush. Again, I think we will be friends, no dating, but a real connection. Mr. Wolf must have heard me because I got several emails from him, and they even contained questions. He REALLY doesn't say much, but time will tell. Mr. Longface is back trying to connect on Yahoo. I don't think either of us have the technology skills we need to even have a chat. And Mr. Bronx finally showed. We didn't have much to say to each other tonight. He told me to take a rest and he would email me later.

I am ready to put <u>Day Four</u> to bed. This entire journey is such a study in the human condition. It remains to be seen as we get closer to <u>Day Thirty</u> how things will play out in the end. I feel like I am looking in on a story with plots and subplots and can't figure out what will happen next. And so, at the end of Day Four, I have one "soulmate," my friend Mr. 45, and a few potential friends. Not bad for someone who hasn't left her room in days! My online experience with the dating scene is still very much that…online. Nothing real and no one to take by the hand or share a moment with. *SIGH.* The night ended with a chat with Mr. Longface. We will talk again, I am sure. I am excited to see how <u>Day Five</u> will turn out.

Chapter 8

AN UNCYNICAL APPROACH

T oday I woke up with mixed feelings. On one hand I am curious about where this is all going because every day is so interesting. On the other hand, I feel so sorry for those great guys, those shy guys who don't think they can find a woman in the face-to-face world, so they succumb to the raw, raunchiness of so many of the women who are online. Some of those guys just give up, and others feel they need to act out their sexual prowess in a chat room to attract a woman, but do they want what they are attracting?

Take Mr. 45 for example. When he first saw me online, he hopped over to my inbox, and as soon as I said hello, he started with the raw sex talk, but there was something about him that came through to me. When I drew him into real conversation, I found that he is an extremely sensitive guy who allows his shyness around women to push him into this distorted online forum. He truly does not believe that he has the ability to make a date with a woman in the real world. He fills his head with scripts about how if he goes up to a woman, her boyfriend will suddenly appear, and the result won't be pretty for any of them.

Oh Mr. 45, how I wish I could help you gain the confidence you need, because you would be a great partner for a woman. You could let your kindheartedness come through. You could focus your deep love and protective nature on a woman you truly love. You could be that funny guy with the quick sense of humor and the ready laugh. You could then have that special someone in your life that would squeal with delight when you show her all that sexual prowess that you now only talk about. How wonderful life could be when you slam the door on those horrid chat rooms and open the door to the real world. You would give yourself the chance to connect with someone, mind, body, and soul. Now all you have is the illusion of a connection and the fantasy of sexual satisfaction – it's sad. Maybe, Mr. 45, there was a reason we met – and that reason isn't for sex. I feel a heart connection to you. I don't know why, but something tells me that if you let me in, I may just be able to help you get out of the online world and find a great, satisfying relationship with a woman. We shall see about all this.

Mr. Pilot is another shy guy with so much to offer. He is quiet, but very well educated and I imagine a pretty good observer of human nature. He knows that online dating is a complete waste of time; yet he, like Mr. 45, is constantly being sucker-punched by his shyness. Doesn't he know how many women have fantasies about men in uniforms? Pilots are often in those fantasies; you know flying high and all. I'm not sure Mr. Pilot will ever let me in enough to talk about these things with him, but we'll see. He does write me long emails – no sex, no raunch and no advances, just decent conversation. I like his approach. He's a solid guy.

Okay, it's time to jump over into my online adventure to see what the day has in store for me. Wow! One quick look in the chat rooms and I've got three new emails. Too bad that all three are smokers, because I don't think I will even respond to them. Mr. Red is an example of what men think women want to hear. I just must share part of his essay with you. Sorry, Mr. Red; this is too much not to share. I need other women to see what's in store for them when they enter the online world. Here are a few words from Mr. Red:

Hi Ladies, I'm on unemployment, so I cant send ya to the moon in that way. I'm layed back, humble, and would like nuthin more than to share passion in all aspects with the right woman. I have much to offer of my experience and insight. Let me learn yers! To teach is to learn twice!

What do you think, Ladies? Are you carried away with that? Well, despite all the spelling errors, I will admit that he is honest about his financial situation, and did express that moment of deep reflection, so if you only want to talk and have sex, Mr. Red is your guy.

Let's see who else has shown up. There is a quick email from Mr. Stamp Collector, and a longer, more passionate email from Mr. Bronx who wants to know if I will share my life with him, and Mr. Longface wants me to take an online IQ test. REALLY? Maybe I should start worrying about what all of this is doing to my personality! Living in the Land of the Warped might not be so good for me after all, but I am committed to following through with this project.

By the end of thirty days, my hope is that I will have a better understanding of this world and come out without becoming cynical. I wouldn't mind having a few new friends and maybe even someone to date, but I don't want to become hardened by being exposed to so many angry people, and worse, so many people who have truly warped minds. It's scary when I think about it too much. I know I am in the safety of my home and my anonymity for the moment, but what happens if I venture out and meet someone? Will they stand me up? Will they be sick or worse, violent? A girl needs to worry about those things. How would it look if I take a bodyguard with me? Seriously, I have been thinking and worrying about all these things.

If I decide to meet someone in a public place, I want to have a friend in that place watching me so I don't get hurt. Sounds romantic, huh? Sorry guys, I watch Criminal Minds too much to not be worried about who you really are. Let's see what's new in my inbox.

Mr. Longface is texting me on Yahoo IM. "Are you there"? "Are you there"? I answer that I have taken the IQ test but can't get the results because I do not want to install new software on my computer. Like a robot he sends me the same three lines of text from before. He isn't reading my answers. I say goodbye. Don't think I could get into a meaningful conversation with him. Should have named him Mr. Robot, but I am sure that name will surface soon.

Mr. Horseman shows up. Sends me a flirt. I reply with a brief hello. He writes a nice email back; upbeat but concerned about the miles between us. I tell him, "Let's just get to know each other online first" I send him a bit more information, but not my name yet.

I see that Mr. Bronx has emailed me again. Still on the "happily ever after" kick and how he would never break my heart if I would only give him a try. I send him a brief reply that we are very far from that discussion, and I am still interested in getting to know him to see if a friendship blooms. Is that a turn-off to a guy, especially from someone who is a "featured" member of an online dating site? I don't know but his kind of "fast and furious" is as scary as the "fast and furious" of a sexual nature. At least he is persistent and writes nice things – nothing vulgar or sexually explicit. I just get this sense that he would be too controlling. I have been far too independent for far too long to say "I do" to shackles. Is there no happy medium?

Ah, I journeyed over to my email and got two new messages. One is from Mr. Bible and one is from Mr. Law of Attraction. Mr. Bible seems like a very nice, very religious widower. Another lonely guy raising the family left behind after the death of his wife. I send him an email. After all, God-fearing is a whole lot better than those who thrive on blasphemy. He lives pretty far away, but that's not necessarily a bad thing.

Now Mr. Law of Attraction might provide me with some good philosophical discussions. That would surely be better than those of Mr. Florida or the Italian Lover. Wow! I am still bringing them up. I think there's a lesson to be learned here. I am looking forward to seeing what Mr. Law of Attraction has to say. He says he has watched "The Secret," something I can at least talk about. He lives very far from me so discussions are all we will have.

It suddenly occurred to me, "Doesn't anyone work anymore?" What are all these guys doing online all day? You might ask the same of me, but at least I am writing a book.

Well, the day has really taken a turn. I now have had 147 emails in five days. I deleted Mr. Longface from my Yahoo IM contact list. He turned into a robot and was very annoying. I also got an email from Mr. BrownEyes. I loved his profile. It was so beautifully written – a man of words and apparently intelligence. I wrote him an email and hope to hear from him again. He even lives in my state. More on that tomorrow.

Mr. Bronx is starting to pique my interest. Every night before bed, he writes me an email. Tonight, his email was over the top and went right into my heart. I need to share just a bit of it so all you women reading this can melt, and you guys can take a lesson:

I wish I could see through your eyes so I would know what you like to see. I wish I knew your wishes, so I could give you everything you want. I wish I dreamed the same dreams you do, and together we could make them come true. I wish I knew what makes you happy, so I could make you the happiest person in the whole world. And lastly, I wish I were a cell in your blood, so I would be sure I was somewhere in your heart.

So right about now, some of you are saying: Oh, come on, he can't be real, and you are right! You, too, can go to LovingYou.com and find quotes on togetherness or love, etc. that you can use to woo your "soulmate," but remember we smart chicks always do our research! I have to give you credit, Mr. Bronx; you did choose a good one, but how will you have a conversation with me when we are together? Will Cyrano de Bergerac be in the wings whispering sweet nothings in your ear so that you can impress me? There is always a price to pay for insincerity.

Mr. Wolf popped back in tonight with his usual one-liners. I answered. I think this is going very slowly with him. I'll bet I am the only one who answers him. Dating, even online dating, is a two-way street, Mr. Wolf. A few new contenders popped in before I was ready to call it a night, Mr. Lack of Technology and Mr. Niceguy. Mr. Lack of Technology claims he can't put a photo online. He doesn't know how. I suggested he ask his kids or friends to help him…doubt if I will hear from him again.

Mr. Niceguy sounds interesting. Speaks several languages and has lived in all kinds of places in the world. That appeals to my love of travel. He is looking for someone who can carry on an intelligent conversation. We'll see if I make the grade. As I put this journal and myself to bed, Mr. Wolf and Mr. Niceguy are neck and neck sending me emails. Wolf and I talk antique cars and car shows and Niceguy loves that I write books and would love to learn how to write one himself. The interesting thing is that he, Mr. Niceguy, is the first person to actually invite me out for coffee or a drink. And Mr. Stamp Collector just sent me a lovely email. He really is a nice man who loves his family. I love this, but this is only <u>Day Five</u>.

Do you believe, as I do, that we attract into our lives that which we need? So far, I am attracting more of the nice guy types my age and less of the "fast and furious" sex mongers. It's a good thing.

Chapter 9

LOOKING FOR THE "LIGHT UP"

My mind is filled with idle chatter as the day begins. I did not answer Mr. Bronx because I think he will be upset if I call him on the fact that he tells me he hates people who lie and cheat; yet, he sends me quotes and pretends they are his own words. Do I act in my usual up-front way, or do I just let it and him go?

I am also thinking of Mr. Niceguy. He is waiting for me to answer him about getting together. This is where all those negative scripts come flooding into my mind. Do I tell him everything that's wrong with me so that he doesn't have to waste his time? Do I muster up the courage to actually go on the date? How do I keep all of those "future" thoughts out of my mind where I am already picturing us as a couple? REALLY??? I can't believe I am even going down this path. I think about his approach: nothing flirtatious at all. He is connecting with me on an entirely different level. He recognizes that I know how to do something that he wants to do, and that interests him. He talks to me about it, complimenting my sense of accomplishment. I like that.

I like his approach because many of the men who have contacted me tell me "How beautiful" I am. They have only seen a photo of my face. Inasmuch as it is a nice face to look at (thanks Mom and Dad), I have had nothing to do with it, other than a little spackle in the morning before going out. When a man tells me I am pretty, although complimented, it doesn't turn me on (well, maybe just a little!), but when he recognizes something in me that I have worked hard to develop, I am all over that. I love when he sees the effects of all the education I have worked hard to get or when he is aware of how positive I am because of all the self-development skills I have learned. That's what turns me on.

It is truly that feeling of "he gets me" that makes me walk with a lighter step and a bigger smile.

Well, it's time to jump over and see what my online day will bring. I think I am beginning to see a pattern here. If I simply jump into a chat room and say nothing for just a brief time and then leave, I suddenly get emails from men who are twenty years my junior. One look and they are on it! They waste no time making an online connection. I rest my case regarding the DNA of the Baby Boomers; they are just not hardwired for technology, nor does it seem, for the "hunt"!

My brief peek into the chat rooms yielded emails from a 40-year-old, a 43-year-old and a 45-year-old who called me a "naughty girl" because I told him I was too old for him. He is persistent and has sent several emails. I am persistent and have told him he needs to play with women his own age.

Mr. Lack of Technology is back with an honest, and of that I am sure, glimpse into who he is. A good education and an interesting sense of humor emerge. I love to spar, so I send him an email back that has some depth and humor. I'd like to have conversations with him. We'll see where that goes.

Mr. Golf is new on the scene. Sent me a one-liner and I answered in the same manner, but with a bit of humor thrown in. Again, we will see where it all goes.

And now Mr. Architect has joined in the mix. I love architects in real life and especially love that he is educated and writes well. One problem is that he is halfway across the country from me! Another pen pal, I guess. He does seem to be a nice man. He is raising his son alone since his wife died several years ago. So many lonely men out there, and yet, with all the single women, no one is making the connections.

The one thing I have learned is that I am too old for chat rooms. It is like learning a new language in hieroglyphics. I have NO IDEA what everyone is saying! I guess I am a dinosaur, after all. The good news is that I don't have to learn it because I am on the clock with this online scene. Twenty-four days to go. I am amazed that I am beginning to pick my favorites and looking for their replies. So, along with my theory on the attributes we assign to people, I also feel that we assign feelings to written communication. I can "read" into a response anything I want to *hear*, and, depending on my mood at the time, I can *feel* all sorts of emotions. I have virtual control over what I want to feel about what each and every person is saying. Or do I? If I were to meet them, would they say those same things in real life that I "hear" them say in an email? I think not.

Mr. Golf is back with an interesting exchange. I think he is also someone who is well-educated. His profile reads "Healthcare" for industry, but my guess is that he is a doctor. Let's see if I am right and if he will reveal that. He has written to me twice but has not yet given me his name.

I have had fabulous, intelligent conversations all day with Mr. Lack of Technology and a beautiful message from Mr. Pilot. I think we are becoming friends. No spark, but really nice exchanges. And then there were the quick exchanges with all the young guys who will reach out to anyone, and I promptly tell them I am old enough to be their mother and that they need to play in another pool. But today there was one who is 36 who needs a mom. He started off as funny, but he has some health problems that really mess up his life. I think there are some things I can suggest to him that will help.

I wonder where Mr. 45 has gone, but I am not surprised when anyone disappears. The online world is very cold. Heck, I have even become a bit cold. I deleted Mr. Longface from my accounts although I see him try to IM me. I don't answer. I think the next person I will need to politely remove myself from is Mr. Bronx, and yes, I did tell him that sending me quotes that he pretended were his words did not sit well with me and made me doubt his sincerity.

So how did <u>Day Six</u> stand up to the other days that have passed? Well, some new players have surfaced, and it has made things so interesting because I've discovered that there are actually some down to earth intelligent men online.

Mr. CountryMusic is a retired teacher, as is Mr. Lack of Technology. Both have great conversations with me. Mr. Stamp Collector is such a lovely man. He sends me great emails, and things are moving forward with Mr. Niceguy. We chatted until the wee hours of the morning. We seem to be able to talk about all sorts of things in a genuine way. And I made a date to meet him in two days! Yes, I did tell him the things about me that I feel are the negatives. He doesn't seem fazed, but of course, he hasn't met me yet! I am sure we can talk books and life. We will talk again tomorrow before we meet.

Mr. Architect is so nice. He sends me down-to-earth emails with just a smattering of the mushy stuff; sweet, but not sickening. I like his personality. I think he might be fun to meet, but he lives so far away. Of all the guys I've talked with in six days, I think he is awesome. The approach of every one of these guys is so different, and yet, their pain comes out.

So, how did the day end? I have had 175 emails in the past six days. I am starting to focus on my favorites, some as friends and some I am attracted to. In case you are keeping score: Mr. Architect, Mr. Pilot, Mr. Lack of Technology, Mr. Stamp Collector, Mr. CountryMusic and Mr. Niceguy are my favorites, and if I think about why, it is because, in every case, they are educated, intelligent men who are also gentlemen. This Baby Boomer Chick hasn't really changed her ideas very much about what she loves. Even in this online tainted world, I still maintain that what's between a man's ears and in his heart are still the most appealing to me!

Chapter 10

GROWING UP THE HARD WAY

When will all the dreams end? Now I wake up each morning thinking about what's going on. All sorts of fantasies start coming into my brain with the light of day.

Last night my conversations with Mr. Niceguy turned a bit personal and intimate, nothing racy, but that deep kind of frank discussion that one can have with a genuine friend. Well, I guess it worked its magic, because without my wanting to go down this road, I am remembering all the nights during my marriage when I longed to feel the warm breath of a man at the nape of my neck as he cuddled with me, or the quaking of my body from the ecstasy of his touch. My eyes cloud over as I think about how I don't want to leave this earth never feeling like a total, sensual woman again. Yet, if I let my mind fast forward a bit more to the "what if," I blush to think that there may be a man out there who could make me feel whole. This is tough.

So what has <u>Day Seven</u> brought me? Well, it started off with an IM discussion with the youngest of my suitors, a boy who is merely 36. He calls me Mom and likes to play but gets very quiet when I take on the role of scolding mother. I am amazed at his tenacity but know that the world is full of people with different ideas about what they like. Sometimes I am so happy that we are not all on the same page.

Mr. CountryMusic is simply a nice guy. I like his words, and his photo shows a lean and handsome guy. He lives far from me, but I wouldn't mind meeting him. I wonder if that thought comes up so easily because I know that it is unlikely.

Is the fantasy world a more comfortable place to live? I think so; no censorship and no stress. Sounds like a good thing to me, but reality has its pull, and I am often whisked, or even slammed, back, hitting with an uncomfortable thud! "Grow up," I tell myself, "This is only a dream. Go back to the endless work and the lack of satisfaction where you have been living for so long."

Well, Mr. Vegan just showed up. Pretty forward guy. Calls me "baby" in the first email and tells me to email him so he can send me some pictures. Well, Mr. Vegan, can't fault you for trying! This online world doesn't come with a manual for success. You have to try everything to see what you are comfortable with and what, with luck, works. I don't feel like your "baby," and P.S. I've cooked for vegans and for those of us who are carnivores. It's hard. I just want a piece of fish or something. I can't eat algae on toast, especially on purpose. I don't know if I am up to answering you back today, Mr. Vegan. Sorry, you caught me at a bad time.

Well, look who is sneaking into my heart; it's Mr. CountryMusic. Did I tell you I don't especially like country music, but I really do like his sensitivity and tenderness? His responses make my heart melt. His answers to my emails resonate with me on a heart-to-heart basis. I think I am going to suggest we start talking on the phone. I am so auditory that the tone and resonance of a man's voice mean a lot to me. There is that certain tone that gets into my bones and sends goosebumps up my arms. It can make me melt long before I feel his touch. It's like those little "love sounds" a man makes when he is caressing you. Well, Mr. CountryMusic, your words are like music to me! If only you didn't live so far away. I would love to take you up on that offer for dinner and drinks the next time I am in your state. And to think I wasn't ever going to respond to you simply because of your ID, and now I feel your friendship. I am anxious to see if you will go the distance and create the opportunity for us to really become friends and maybe more. Just the thought of that makes me smile.

Wow just checked my email and got the cutest note from Mr. Cutiepie wanting to know if I was from this planet since he has never seen anyone so beautiful. He tells me to keep smiling because my smile is so radiant. Nice job, Cutiepie, you made me smile even more! And yes, I will send you one of my quick, banter-type replies; you are just too cute not to answer.

Well, the day has progressed into Mr. CountryMusic picking up my spirits and then throwing me against a wall as soon as I told him I was not interested in marriage. Wow! One message says, "Let me be your shoulder if you need one to lean on," and "You would make a beautiful bride," and when I tell him, "No marriage talk," he says, "Okay, goodbye!"

Mr. Niceguy is progressively making deep conversation with me. We both seem to be able to talk about the hurtful things in our lives as well as the meaningful ones. I like talking with him and have agreed to have lunch with him. So, I guess this is to be considered my first date. I am scared and excited all at once.

Mr. Lack of Technology popped online to ask how my day was going. He seems down, no intellectual conversation. Baby Boy popped back on IM. He is so funny and quirky. He loves older women. I am sure he will move on soon since he is getting no advances from me. Really, I am old enough to be his mom, although he tells me his real mom is 72 and dates a 50-year-old. No wonder he likes older women; his mom has taught him an interesting lesson on age differences.

The day ends with a very long video chat with Mr. Niceguy. He wants me to hear his voice and recognize his face before we meet for lunch tomorrow. As I am talking with him, Cutiepie pops up over and over on IM chat. Not a patient man at all. He vows to love me forever. He wants me to get International Calling Service for my phone so that we can talk, because he happens to be traveling to Africa on business. He tells me he will meet me next week; money is no object, as he is rich! Okay, now my guard is really up. I wonder when he will ask me to buy something for him because he can't get it where he is. And the night ends with emails and photos of two new contenders: Mr. California and Mr. Irish. Both have lost their wives, and both are sure that God sent me to them. They live on opposite sides of the US from each other, and yet they will both read me scriptures every night, and, wouldn't you know it, they each have teenage daughters.

Chapter 11

WHAT ABOUT THE DATE?

Today, my thoughts turn to a movie that came out in 2010 called "Up In the Air" with George Clooney. There is a scene in the movie where a woman tells George that her boyfriend just broke up with her in an email. An email! It sounds preposterous and oh so wrong on every level. Fast forward to today and an email break up would be an improvement over the total lack of response one gets when your virtual suitor pours his heart out to you with poetry stolen from an online source and the promise of life ever after, and in the next moment no response at all.

Well, Mr. Cutiepie asks me to call him. When I tell him I can't, he asks for my number. He calls me so I can hear his voice because, "Baby, you are my everything. Do you have a passport? Will you come to Spain to meet me? What would you like me to buy you?" I laugh to myself. I remember the expression, "If it looks like s##t and smells like s##t and tastes like s##t, it must be s##t!" He sends me poetry again and is quite irritated when I do not reply immediately.

BabyBoy keeps popping up. Needs attention and wants to know when I can chat. Not until extremely later, I say, remembering my date. Mr. Lack of Technology pops up again to thank me for suggesting he get out and do something fun. It worked, and he is feeling and sounding better. Mr. Stamp Collector sends me his phone number and asks for mine. He wants to talk.

Mr. Cutiepie chats for a while, calls me five times, and then asks me to buy him something from the states. There it is – the scam. I tell him I can't, and he suddenly has to go to sleep. We'll see if he ever shows up again.

So get on, you must be saying, "What about the date?"

Mr. Niceguy greets me with a hug and kiss. "What, no flowers?" I had the fleeting idea that he might have brought me some, or was that just my hope of a fantasy world? He looks older than I thought but has a nice voice and blue eyes. We have lunch and talk easily, very easily. As we leave the restaurant, he has his arm around me and suggests we sit in the car and talk. And I know what you're thinking, but we were in the restaurant's parking lot in the middle of the day for heaven's sake. What did you think we would be doing??? Honestly!

We talk for hours and then he suggests that we go on another date next week. He is so easy to talk with and has such a gentle voice and touch that I decide to say yes. I am excited to be seeing him again. I liked the way he held my hands and caressed them ever so gently when we talked. No pressure and lots of connection. It was really a good day.

Chapter 12

BEING A GOOD FRIEND

Cutiepie is back on IM. This time he has been robbed and his son is in a coma. Will I send him money for oxygen? Wow, I thought the scam was that he wanted me to buy his son a game from the US. Was I ever wrong! OXYGEN! What happened to the millions of dollars he professed to have? Even if I were to be ridiculous enough to wire him money, his son would be long gone before my money arrived! He is angry with me and thinks I am really cold. His son is in a coma, for goodness sakes. I tell him I must go.

Mr. Lack of Technology sends me an upbeat note. We have been talking quite a bit online, but he never even suggests that we meet or phone. I am relieved about that but like the depth of our conversations. He's smart, a retired teacher who can actually carry on a conversation that doesn't start with the word "Baby."

Mr. Stamp Collector and I finally talk on the phone. He is a nice guy, but, and I don't want to sound like a real snob, I don't think he and I have been exposed to the same things in life. He seems to have extremely simple and modest tastes. I lean more to the finer things. At least there was nothing provocative in our conversations.

Online later in the evening (yes, even I go out on occasion), there are some flirts and a few messages from an entirely new set of suitors! In eight days I have received 232 emails. I sent emails to Mr. Architect to tell him "love" should not even enter into the picture yet. I also tried nicely to tell the two men who will be reading me scripture every night that they will be vastly disappointed in me when they try to teach me the Word of God. I bet they try again anyway.

And new on the scene is Mr. Cruise. Well, he is already deeply in love with me from my profile and of course that fabulous picture of me! He has to talk with me after he pours out his heart. Did I tell you that he, too, is in Africa, has a daughter and has lost his wife? He joins me on Yahoo IM and we talk for a while. His notes are long and deep, but I sense a new plot will unfold since he isn't an American citizen. I wonder if he needs a ticket to the states. Ah, do I sound cynical yet? And it's only <u>Day Eight.</u>

Mr. Niceguy and I chatted on the phone and decided to move our date up to earlier in the week. We both want to see each other sooner rather than later. Too soon to know what will develop, but I really like his gentleness and the tender way he cradles my face in his hands and gives me the tiniest kisses on the eyelids, the cheeks and then the lips. He is a good suitor. He really knows how to treat a woman, the kind that could win your heart.

Ladies, please listen up! If you know a guy who is talking about going onto an online dating site, please be a good friend and take his picture! Honestly, what are some of them thinking with those photos? Some of the mug shots are taken at such close range you can see their nose hairs. Scary, dark or overly sappy photos just don't turn women on. Ladies, I implore you; help those guys out! Be a good friend.

Before <u>Day Eight</u> comes to a close, both Mr. Irish and Mr. California come back even though I tell them I am not as religious as they are. New on the scene is the General. He's in the Army. His note sounds more genuine than most. He wants my email so that he can send me some photos. My assumption is that he will be interesting to chat with. I am getting obnoxiously brazen. I have already warned him that I do not respond well to men who promise me love everlasting on the second email. Oh, well, this is the virtual world, after all.

In the wee hours of the morning Mr. Bonsai shows up to give me a poem:

Some people come into our lives and quietly go. Others stay for a while and leave footprints on our hearts and we are never the same. But the beauty of life does not depend on how happy you are, but on how happy others can be because of you. To the world you might be one person, but to one person you might just be the world.

Okay, Mr. Bonsai, you have captured my attention. In email two you are asking me if I like to dance and do I go to concerts. Sounds like you "just wanna have fun." Ah, it has been too long. Can't remember when the last time was that I went to a concert and danced. Have I really gotten so old that I have stopped living? The time slipped away when I wasn't looking. I was stuck being married and couldn't pursue those fun events alone, nor could I seek out a partner. Mr. Bonsai has made me nostalgic for those carefree days when I could gather up a group of friends and go out. I loved his poem and his spirit. We'll see what develops tomorrow.

Chapter 13

HORNY

Let's see, shall we make a list of the players still on the scene?

Mr. Lack of Technology is still writing to me. I like his notes, but there is absolutely no hint of meeting or dating.

Mr. Stamp Collector is also writing notes, more banal than those of Mr. Lack of Technology, but I don't mind being his pen pal for a while. He's a lonely man.

Mr. Niceguy is crawling into my heart. We have moved our date up again to tomorrow. I am excited, and he seems to be as well.

Mr. Irish is also on the scene, as well as the General. I would say that I am far more connected intellectually and spiritually to the General, but he is far more physically fit than I am. That may turn out to be the deal breaker. He is wonderful to talk with. No hint of lust. He is smart and allows his heart and head to come out in his notes to me. And he is tall, dark and handsome! Dare I hope?

Back on the scene and totally confusing to me is Mr. CountryMusic. Why did he slam me against the virtual wall when I said, "no marriage?" Didn't he ignore my follow-up note to say I just wanted to be friends? Now he is back to sending me one-liners every day.

Mr. Bonsai is still with me. He lives an active life – that's good! I can probably help him with a bit of career coaching. We'll see where this will go. He initially sounded like he would be asking me out for a date but hasn't yet.

Very late in the evening, I checked online to see who was on IM and saw that Mr. 45 was there. I hadn't seen him in a few days and decided to say "hi." "Tired," he says, "can't talk long."

"Horny," he says, "how about you?" Well, I have never been asked that and don't know what to say. Am I "horny"? Will I allow myself to even think about it? How do I reply?

I told you Mr. 45 was going to be my ethical dilemma. I get really turned on by the sound of his voice. I muster up my courage and say, "Me, too." "Call me," he says. "Do you want to play?" And at that very moment, late in the night, I didn't have a single thought about propriety or age, or even body image; I simply called him. We played on the phone until we were both giggling with ecstasy. So. this is what having a friend with benefits means! I drifted off to sleep, smiling at the turn of events, thinking that I might not be as cynical about this online dating as I thought. I doubt that Mr. 45 will ever be reading me the scriptures!

Chapter 14

FINDING ALL THE PARTS OF YOU

Woke up to find a long, beautiful email from the General. I wonder why I like him so soon. I sense that he won't be playing those useless games that promise sexual favors or a life of endless joy. I think he might just be the real deal. He is smart, and you know how turned on I get with a man's brain, but he is also warm and deep in the way he responds to my emails. I write him a long email and tell him about the real me. I don't pretend to be Barbie. I don't flirt or show the sexy side of me in any way. I simply write from the heart.

When I analyze how I feel about all the men I have been in touch with online over the past ten days, I realize that, although I love to spar with words and even let it become a bit spicy on the rare occasion, what I really want in this warped world is to be authentically connected to a man with whom I can share myself completely. I want someone with whom I can be the intellectual me, the serious me, the funny me, the goofy me and even the sexy me.

Wow! It might be easier to stop a war than it will be to find all that in a man, but a girl can dream, can't she? I am looking forward to hearing back from the General if he decides that my honesty is worth more than the things I lack. I am also looking forward to date number 2 with Mr. Niceguy.

I emailed Mr. Lack of Technology. It is the first time I have done the reaching out. I like his brain! I have had over 250 emails from men in the last ten days and the story is still unfolding. It is quite the ride on the Ferris wheel of life! My emotions and the ensuing hopes attached to them go up and down, up and down.

Well, Mr. Niceguy took me to the movies and out to dinner. I had forgotten the sweet tenderness of sitting in a dark movie theater with a man's arm around my shoulders and the touch of his hands on mine. He is so gentle and tender, giving me an occasional kiss and caressing my hands. Oh, how I had forgotten all of this, and it feels so good. At dinner we share a meal. I love that. We talk so easily. He constantly reaches over the table and caresses my face gently in his hands. He tells me he can't stop touching me! I blush to think where this might be going and if I am ready. It's refreshing that he seems so patient and oh so gentle.

After dinner we go to his car to talk. I know what you're thinking; there's the car thing again! We sit in the back seat and laugh because, at our age, back seat dating is only a funny memory. It can no longer be a reality... bad backs, bad knees, and the like, now strongly come into play here! We sit and talk and cuddle and kiss for hours and hours! I like this guy. I never expected to really meet anyone who would be this patient and respectful. I like having time to decide where I want to go with this. We spend hours like this, wrapped in each other's embrace. I went home so happy and feeling so connected to another human being.

As I reflect, I think people come into our lives for a reason. We don't always know why, but often they are just what we need. I think Mr. Niceguy is just what I needed as my first encounter with a man after a bad marriage.

I feel so lucky that he is loving and patient as I wrap my head around these experiences. I go to sleep smiling and knowing I will sleep well for the first time in a very long time!

Chapter 15

HEAD GAMES

Woke up thinking how different my life is after only eleven days. I am happier, more introspective. And I'm dating! Mr. Niceguy can't wait to see me again. "When can we meet?" he asks over and over. Okay, so maybe his patience is wearing a bit thin, but he has been a gentleman thus far.

Baby Boy is chatting with me. He is starting to be much more real, not feeling the need to shock me with his quirky ideas.

Mr. Lack of Technology is persisting still, but this time he ends his email with the question, "Still interested?" This is the first move in all these days toward anything that even remotely resembles dating. We'll see. I would hate to break up a good daily exchange of words for all the complicated dating that might ensue!

Mr. Bonsai seems to imply that I am too accomplished for him, what with the book writing and all. No more talk of concerts and dancing. Too bad; that sounded like fun!

I check my email and check again, hoping the General will get back to me. Although usually a very patient woman, I am disillusioned. I was so hoping to get to know him better.

New on the scene is Irishman2. The interesting thing is that he is the third man to send me the exact same email! Something's fishy here. I'll let you decide for yourselves, Ladies, at least be forewarned:

> *Hello sweet honey, thanks for the mail. I know you not surprised to receive an email like this from me. In fact, the world will be a better place if we have people like you around us. I'm also alone and looking for someone to share my whole life with, not just someone, but one who have all the good characters in life. I'm of that type and want someone with the same to spend with. I can see you are of that type because you stated it in your advert the type of person of you want. I really know what love is and the type who give his whole heart in a relationship. Relationships are built one day at a time; they take time, patience, honesty, passion, and ability to compromise and grow! So with true love, is by sharing bad and good times together. True love is a covenant that we build on a strong foundation and that's why we don't develop it within a day. It takes some time to mature and that's when both sees that they are having the same strong feeling for each other. It is with true love as it is with ghosts; everyone talks about it, but few have seen it. I promise to make my one and only the most happiest woman on earth if only she is willing to accept me as part of her. I'll be there whenever she needs me and promise never to do anything to hurt her feeling. I'll love her just the way she is, being blind, disable, deaf or dumb or whatever category that she falls in. I really mean my words and I'm serious too. I'm ever ready to sail to the end of the sea with her and ever prepared to do anything to have her forever. I promised to be the man of her dreams cus I'm not going to let her down on earth or hurt her feelings, since the adage goes, A*

man without a woman is like a river or a stream without a source and as relationships are built on trust and with mutual respect I assure him my whole heart. I don't know and can't tell if that special person is you, but I believe it's you cus your advert alone speaks of it all so why don't we give ourselves a chance and find out what happens. I know at this point, there is the need for me to say something about myself so you can know the kind of person you talking to. Pls don't let the distance drives you away from me, who knows if I am your lost rib you have been looking for. Just be patient, have faith and then fix my rib on your lost rib to see if it's suit with your body. I hope to hear from you soon my dear one.

There it is the profession of love and life happily ever after with the man from whom I was molded. I really do need to know where all these guys are shopping for email templates. Maybe I can start a new business writing love templates for men! I hope they didn't pay much for this one because there isn't one shred of good grammar contained in that document!

I get a sweet text from Mr. Niceguy. "When can I see you?" "Don't forget me." A short while later, he calls me. Hates to bother me when I am working, but really can't stop thinking about me. The funny thing is that I feel the same! I don't commit to a new date yet, but probably will tomorrow. This new part of my life is getting in the way of my work. How do other people manage dating and working?

A few new emails come in. There are almost too many characters in this play to talk about. I like the ones who have remained for a variety of reasons. The effects of all these characters on me are interesting. It is fun to see the range of emotions I have as I am brought up and down, simply by the written word.

Mr. Lack of Technology has emailed me twice today. He is softening and tells me how he is cooking for his critically ill neighbor and her son. I compliment him on revealing his sweeter side. I like that he did. I hear from him again later in the day. He has recently started asking about my life. He thinks I have lots of energy, which I do. Again, absolutely no advances, but I know he likes sparring with me as much as I do with him.

Mr. Niceguy is missing me and sends me a message that dinner was almost perfect, but one thing was missing - me. He wants to know when he can see me. We make plans to spend an entire Saturday together. I am looking forward to it.

The General finally wrote to me. I am so excited. He loved my email and wants to get to know me. I can only breathe a sigh of relief that he did not push my email aside. I really want to get to know him. I don't know why I am so attracted to him, the brain, the respectful emails, the uniform, his profession? Who knows, but time will reveal all. He will be home in a few months and with any luck we will have exchanged enough emails and have talked on Skype enough to have some understanding of each other.

I still think this online world is pretty much a head game. Who knows if the scripts in your head are the same as those of the other person? Are you really reading the words as they were meant to be read, or are you projecting your desired outcome on the printed word? I have noticed that I have stopped watching Criminal Minds while I am going through the motions of finding that special someone. The online world is a bit scary, and I don't need to fill my head with scary ideas about criminals and murderers while I am trying to decide whether or not a person is genuine. I have enough going on in my head without adding the seamier side of human nature to my thoughts.

Today was a turning point in many ways. Mr. Niceguy called and asked if he could see me. What happened to our Saturday date? Today is only Tuesday. We meet and drive to the beach to look at the water, only I never see the water. We hug and kiss for hours. He is just so gentle and hasn't tried to force me into anything. We have fun talking. We have fun kissing.

Mr. Lack of Technology wrote me a note to tell me he finds me both interesting and exciting. He is looking for a friend and a lover. He asks about my libido. The only problem is that he never posted a photo, so I have no idea what he looks like. I lob the ball back into his court. Sight unseen is unheard of. I need to see what he looks like first. I don't want to lose my sparring partner, only to gain an unsatisfying relationship. We'll see if he sends me his photo and asks me on a real date.

The General continues to write. I like him and hope he is as nice in real life. He excites me. I am amazed at how sincere and honest he sounds. I guess he's the type who doesn't have time for ridiculous head games. Just the facts, Jack, but can he laugh, and can he love? Still, he looks really sexy in that uniform! I wake up every morning eager to see if he has written to me again. He writes long emails and gives me the sense that he is anxious to keep our correspondence going so that we can develop a relationship. My anticipation is palpable. I have written to many men, but there is something very different about this one. I can wait. I think he just may be worth it!

The night ended in an unexpected way. Mr. Niceguy called and wanted to meet me. We had already spent several hours together earlier in the day, so I was very surprised. I agreed and thirty minutes later, we were locked in each other's arms. He is such an amazing kisser. He can do things with his mouth…well, I blush to think of it! Every time I thought I was ready to leave, I found that I couldn't. I am so drawn to his tenderness. I love that he doesn't pressure me for sex, but holds me, caresses me and kisses me like I am something exquisitely precious. He melts my heart.

Chapter 16

IS IT CHEATING?

This morning I woke up feeling like a teenager. When I looked in the mirror my hair was all tousled and I looked ten years younger. It was so much fun to be treated like a desirable woman yesterday. There are a few emails this morning from new characters. I haven't answered them yet because Baby Boy is ready to chat. He is still looking for a way to meet. I like that he is holding great conversations. I laugh a lot with things that he says. We talk business quite a bit. He suggests we talk again about the possibility of my working for him. We'll see about that. He is lots of fun as a sparring partner; he has a good way with words and banters back quickly… just what I love.

Mr. Niceguy comes on to chat. He is still purring over last night. Very sweet and still very patient with me. We chat for a while, and he asks if I can meet him after work later today. I hadn't planned to, but it sure sounds like a good idea. Maybe we can see a movie.

Another new character is on the scene. Mr. Artist has written me a formal note that includes how beautiful and photogenic I am. He would love to invite me out if I am available. We'll see if he ever writes back. There are a few others, but I don't think they will last long...too many to actually count.

Mr. Niceguy takes me to the movies. It was lots of fun. We stayed wrapped in each other's arms in the theater, and it felt good. After the show, we went outside and sat in the car. He surprised me by bringing a thermos of hot tea and cookies! There in the back seat of the car we had a picnic and hugged and kissed until the wee hours of the morning. We are getting closer emotionally and physically. It will be hard to break away from him if I need to. I am beginning to yearn for his touch and his gentle kisses. I am trying to protect his heart, after all, but he seems to be falling in love with me. It's too soon, and I am relieved that he is not demanding sex.

I can't allow myself to jump into the first experience wholeheartedly. I guess the bottom line is that I want to be certain that it is right, and because I like two other men that I haven't yet met in person, I feel I should explore that as well.

Chapter 17

EFFECTS OF ANONYMITY

I missed my chat with Baby Boy this morning. He makes me laugh and starts my day off right. Hopefully, we will talk later. He desperately wants to meet me, but I am reticent because he loves older women. I don't want to just be a category to him.

Mr. Niceguy called me. "Can we meet tonight? I miss you." I told him no. I need some rest. We will meet Friday night and take a long country drive all day Saturday. My thoughts go to a sad place. I see the love and adoration in his eyes and in his gentle touch and I worry that if I feel he isn't the one, he will be hurt. This is hard. He has been so nice to me, and we have developed a closeness. I have seen him nearly every day since we met. He has been a wonderful experience for me. I like the way he thinks. I like that he treats me like a lady. I like that he always cradles my face in his hands and gives me butterfly kisses on my cheeks and nose and eyelids. I like that he takes care of me and brings me picnics. However, I think that I may simply not be ready to move into an intimate relationship.

The General wrote me a long letter. I seem to wait in anticipation for those letters and worry when they don't come quickly. He is very serious and direct.

I try to send him upbeat and fun responses with a bit of raw honesty thrown in. I like him and can only hope that I will like him as much in real life. I won't get to meet him for several months. Somehow, he makes me want to be a better person. It is interesting to feel that way after only a few emails. He has impeccable character...how refreshing! I hope he also has a fun side, because I certainly do, and another lopsided relationship just won't work for me! I send him long emails in return. I try to send stories of my adventures that I think will make him laugh. He talks of wanting to grow our relationship and how nice it will be to spend time together. I bet it will. He is a precious gem, and the kind of man who would be a great partner. I can only hope that we have the chemistry needed to sustain a relationship.

Mr. Bonsai pops in every day with an email that says "Have a nice day." No longer does he suggest dancing. Sorry, Mr. Bonsai, I would have loved to dance! If you just need a pen pal for a short while, I guess I can continue to send you one-liners, but was it good for you??? Mr. Lack of Technology isn't beating around the bush any longer. He wants me to know that if there is a meeting and we have a physical chemistry beyond our intellectual chemistry, then off to the bedroom it will be. Too old to spend the rest of life celibate! Well, I must admit, he has a point there.

I like a person who is direct, but I still maintain that the anonymity of the online forum allows for the type of directness that we so lack in our tactful world. If we were face to face, would either of us, in fact, be able to say, 'Well, we know we are intellectually compatible, and I sense that we have a physical chemistry, so let's live in a world filled with endless lovemaking?' I doubt it.

It reminds me of the movie with Jim Carrey and another with Ricky Gervais where neither one could lie. It is a funny concept, especially for the online world where lying is the rule! Online we choose who we want to be. What sports do you enjoy? Why isn't couch potato on the list? How tall are you and what do you weigh? The drop-down menu doesn't contain choices like skeletally thin or morbidly obese, so what's a person to choose if they are those things? And what about the sexual deviants? Where is the box for them to check off?

In the virtual world, I can be anything I want to be! The beauty of it all is that I can be a different character every single day, or I can become the multi-personality Cybil type where I can play a different role on each of the different singles websites. Why, I don't have to even be single!

So when Mr. Lack of Technology suggests a meeting and I have never even laid eyes on a photo of him, I get scared, and the beauty of the virtual world is that I can tell him that. No photo? Quasimodo's face comes to mind and I shudder! I need more before I will meet you in person. You are a really smart guy, Mr. Lack of Technology; you should know that! Once again, the ball is in his court, but this time, I think he will play, and maybe I am just a bit excited about that. I love his intelligence and the way he can spar with me. If he is as eloquent in person and if he is physically attractive to me, it will be fun to get to know him.

My anticipation is growing as the relationships with three men start to unfold. I don't want to hurt any of them, and yet, this is the first time I have felt that there is a chance that I could find someone with whom I am compatible and for whom I am the world. Wouldn't that be refreshing! There is, of course, always the possibility that I will lose them all, and there is even the possibility that I will fall in love with them all. They are all so very different. Each has a special quality that thrills me. I worry a lot about all this. I want to be able to openly love a man, but what if he rejects me, or what if he turns out to be the one and I have to let the other two down. I can't bear the thought of ever hurting any of them, and, if at all possible, I hope not to be hurt, as well.

Mr. Niceguy calls and says that he can't stand not seeing me tonight, and although we both need some rest, I decide to go out with him. We are growing very close. We talk and hold each other for hours. I see the way he cherishes me. I love the way he looks at me and gives me advice. I am growing fond of him, too. I love spending time together, just talking and holding each other tight. It soothes me and makes me feel complete. I especially love that he never pressures me for physical intimacy. He has remained a gentleman throughout our relationship.

Before I go to sleep, I write another note to the General. I want him to always go to sleep and wake up with an email from me. I love writing stories to help him forget where he is. I can only try to bring him something to smile about until he comes home, and we meet. I love all that he stands for: the values, the honesty, the hard work, the rock-solid nature and the stability. I don't know whether or not we will have any chemistry when we meet, but so far our online correspondence is going well.

Chapter 18

BUYER BEWARE

Every day is a complete surprise in the online world. In fifteen days, I have had 275 emails from men who just want to find a good woman. It's sad, especially for those nice, shy guys who truly believe that they can't find anyone. As a woman, I am starting to think that I have been wrong my entire life about how to get a date. I am from the era of mindset which keeps women from asking guys out. I now think it's hogwash! Ladies, if you see a shy guy, go up to him and make small talk. He may just be too shy. Don't be too forward because they are easily scared by too much confidence or the hint of too much emotion at once, but those shy guys really wake up when they feel safe.

Well, today Mr. Lack of Technology gave me a sucker punch! He dropped me with the speed of a gazelle. I must have hit a pain point. Maybe he does look like Quasimodo, but for some reason, I suddenly remind him of his wife. (I guess she's not an "ex" yet!) He cordially wishes me well and hopes we part friends. Well, there it is; the virtual world at its best! Door slams and conversation ends in a flash. You get no chance for rebuttal. You get silence, just silence. Cut off with no explanation or the hope of one. Sure, Mr. Lack of Technology, have a good life, we'll be "friends" forever! I am a bit sad over the loss of my sparring partner. Mr. Lack of Technology was so smart, and I really loved having those weighty emails to enjoy. Not a fluff type of guy, but deep with a bit of funny sarcasm thrown in. I think he went too deep into his feelings and when he looked around; he remembered it was the virtual world. How could he say all those things, draw out similar emotions from me, and never meet face-to-face?

It was too personal and much too soon for those discussions: We never should have gone there, but that's the trap that is so easy to fall into in the virtual world. You let down your guard. You feel a sense of "protection" in the virtual world: no supposition of rejection until it hits you in the face!

Mr. Lack of Technology is a perfect example of a person who got caught up in the "freedom of speech" trap that the virtual world is known for. Once you have said, or rather "typed" your true feelings, there is no delete button. Not only is it out there for your online sparring partner to read, but it has both the potential and the capacity to be out there for the world to read!

He was smart to keep his "Quasimodo" face hidden to the virtual world, a bit of respectful anonymity, but he certainly ran for the hills when he realized that not only did he heat things up, but he got me heated up as well. He ran scared, and in the virtual world that's much easier to do than in the real world where the other person knows where you live and what you look like. They can pursue you and may just get another chance.

In the virtual world, silence, just cold, dark silence. Where on this online dating site was the "buyer beware" statement? When I paid my money to play in this pool, nowhere did I read that my heart could be broken in the coldest of ways.

There should be a warning for that!

Now who is left to break my heart? Well, there's the General, who will always be the upstanding guy. What I know about him is that I love his sense of responsibility and the feeling that I could always count on his word being his bond. What I don't know is whether or not, if we became a couple, he could rock my world physically. I am looking for that body-mind-soul connection. I wonder if that's really too much to ask from one man.

Mr. Niceguy certainly would have the capacity to rock my world and melt my heart. I find that I am trying to keep my heart safe because I could fall very hard for him. "Too soon," I keep telling myself. "You are unprepared for a love affair at this point."

Baby Boy is really starting to turn my head, now that he has been having real discussions with me. I like the way he thinks…really smart and a fabulous businessman. He also has a caring heart. So, the dilemma is his age. How do I get over that? It won't ever change, and I know that as I age, it will be more and more obvious. He's too young. I don't want to play with his heart. He would love a woman like me: reliable, successful, smart, and kind-hearted. I want that for him, but I don't know if it should come from me because of the age thing. At least he has already been married once. I would really feel horrible if he hadn't had that experience. I couldn't be his first relationship. Well, I don't even want to go there. We are just talking.

I went on a day-long date with Mr. Niceguy. It was so relaxing. He and I drove for hours to the northwest corner of the state, talking and holding hands. I am noticing how electrified my body is when he puts his hand on my knee. We talk about life and our individual philosophies. We talk about each other and how we are beginning to feel about spending time together. He is soft spoken. He is loving and never hurried, seems to have the capacity to wait until I am ready. He seems to know that I will be ready for all of him someday. We stop to have the picnic he has brought me. I have never had a man make a picnic for me. I have always been the provider of food and fun in a relationship. I kind of like this, but the cynical side of me says, "How long would that last if we were a couple?"

We leisurely drive back. We decide to go somewhere where we can spend some alone time. I am hooked. I love the long, tender kisses he gives me that touch my soul. How do I resist that? What I see for the first time is a new look. He is falling in love with me. He keeps reminding me that I have had a hard life, and it's about time I did something just for me. Is he the man for me? I love that he not only makes me feel special, but he also makes me feel beautiful; it's in his eyes, in his touch and in his words. We spend hours in warm embraces. "Not ready," I say to his longing advances. "Okay, I'll wait," he replies, "but I really want to be one with you." We kiss for a very long time, wrapped in each other's arms, tongues telling a story to each other. Soulful, deep kisses that are unhurried and oh so loving. I am hooked, so very hooked!

"I love you," he whispers, "and I think you love me, too. You and I need each other. I have never felt so whole in my life. You are an amazing woman. You are beautiful, you are so accomplished, you can carry on a great conversation, and you are so sensual."

I started a new exercise regime. Every day, three times a day, I stand in front of the mirror and say out loud, "Protect your heart, protect your heart, protect your heart." Do you think it's working??? I don't think so. My heart is already his, but I keep waiting for the other shoe to fall. I don't know why, but I feel that something is going to go wrong. I can't believe I could be this happy. I can't believe I wasted so many years in a loveless relationship. What was I thinking?

Did I think I would live forever, or even long enough to find happiness? I don't even trust happiness when I find it! How sad is that? I find a man who is my match in many ways and I can't trust my happiness. I think that tells me I need to give myself time, or maybe I am just scared. Happiness is a new concept. I don't know how to deal with it.

———————————————————————

There are a few new characters in this play. Some sound interesting, and I hope to get an opportunity to at least explore who they are and what they stand for. Mr. Conditions knows exactly what he wants and doesn't want. His profile spans paragraph after paragraph. It looks like a Chinese menu filled with all he desires in a woman. Good luck with that, Mr. Conditions. I emailed him; we'll see if he responds.

There is also Mr. 46 who thinks age doesn't matter if love is there. I think it matters, except regarding friendship. I don't know if I even want to answer him, maybe tomorrow.

Also new on the scene are Mr. Lack of Commitment and Mr. Swift. It's funny how simply by reading their profiles you can get a sense of who they are. Take Mr. Lack of Commitment, for example. Did you think the ladies wouldn't see the red flag when you put down that you are 61 years old and haven't yet been married? What does that instantly tell me…hence the name. His profile says life should be fun and filled with travel. No time for a serious relationship, I think. We'll see. He might never write back because he can't commit to even an online relationship.

Mr. Conditions seems like he would be a better match for me. Sounds smart. I liked his profile but wondered if it is just my love of words and the fact that he uses so many that interest me. What if his profile is all there is, like the movie trailers that are the best of the movie and such a disappointment?

The thing I think is funny is that so many men reach out with a flirt or a brief hello email, and when I answer, they never write back. Heck, I'm not giving them my deepest secrets or my philosophy of life; I usually just say hello, thanks for writing. What does that really say about them, or the vibes I am giving off? This has certainly become a psychological study on the dating habits of the sexes.

Mr. 45 popped on IM to say, "Hi, Lover girl." I am still embarrassed about that one but will always like this guy. There is something special about him. I am comfortable talking with him and feel that his feelings match mine. That may be weird, but I have enjoyed what we've shared, embarrassment and all. I never thought I would think that a little online fun would be an experience that I could enjoy. So maybe, just maybe, my attitude regarding the online world is beginning to soften. Aren't we all just spirits looking for connections on many different levels? Can there ever be anything more wonderful than that feeling of belonging and connectedness that comes from sharing something intimate with another human being. Thanks, Mr. 45 for a moment of joy – no strings attached!

Mr. Swift is just that; he is immediately ready to meet. He wants to know why I left so soon and doesn't like my one-liner response. Wants to know what I want to do. What's the plan? I answer photo first, emails, phone call and then, if things go well, we will meet. Let's see if I am too slow for Mr. Swift.

Mr. Bonsai is back! He's going to a concert (without me) and wants to know what I am planning to do today. There is an expression, "What you do once is what you always do." Mr. Bonsai, although nice, is not an action type of guy, or maybe it's a ploy to make me want to see him! So far, I doubt that. Oh well, another pen pal, and for now, with the way I have already messed up my heart, a pen pal is enough. We'll see if in the end, Mr. Bonsai falls into that virtual black hole like so many of the others!

I talked with Mr. Niceguy. "Do you have time for me tonight?" I agree, knowing full well that I am getting deeper and deeper into this relationship. I anticipate his eyes adoringly looking at me and the electricity his touch brings. I know that by just hearing his voice, I turn to mush. What am I doing? I am barely out of my marriage; this is no time to move right into a new relationship, or is it? We go to the movies. He sits with his arm around my shoulders holding my hand. I feel good. Every once in a while, he gently lifts my chin up and gives me a soulful kiss. His eyes look at me with love and adoration.

"Are you okay, Sweetie?" he whispers. I want to scream, "I love this man!" After the movies, we go out to have coffee. He reaches across the table and takes my hands, cupping them between his. He looks deep into my eyes. "I need to tell you something," he says. Ladies, you know where this is going, don't you?

And there, in that moment, he shatters my heart in a most unexpected way. "I am married, and my wife has been away. She will be back next week."

You could have scraped me up off the floor.

He goes on and on about how we can still see each other, and he will always be my friend. He loves me. I believe he does. I thought Mr. 45 was going to be my ethical dilemma, but I was so wrong! What do I do with this information? I love him, but this is wrong on so many levels. For me, continuing this relationship, knowing he is married, would be the lowest thing I could do. My heart hurts instantly. How can this be fair? What did I do to deserve this? All I wanted was a moment of happiness after so many years of pain. I thought I had found that happiness in this man, this wonderful man who was so tender and compassionate, and who really gave me some loving advice.

Do I have a choice? I don't think so. I will be forever hurt, but I can't keep up a relationship with a man who not only is married, but who will never divorce his wife because he respects her enough to let her live in the "security" of marriage. I wonder if she ever suspected this. I wonder how many times this has happened before. I wonder how much more pain my heart can take.

I feel broken on so many levels. The sad thing is that, no matter what your ideas are about men who cheat on their wives, I can tell you that he is sad, too. He may have started out thinking he would have a fling, but in the end, he was very distraught over my decision to not see him. I couldn't be that woman who knowingly would take another woman's man. There could be no amount of pain in my heart that would convince me otherwise. I wasn't angry with him; I was simply sad and longing for the connection I had felt with him, his touch, his kisses, and most of all the loving way he wanted to protect me. We were both hurting – no happy ending here, just pain.

Chapter 19

ARE DATING SITES FOR NON-DATERS?

The day started off early with a provocative chat from Baby Boy. He has certainly softened towards me, as I have him. It's interesting how over the course of just a few days, I have grown fond of him and look forward to his chats. This morning he is happy that he woke up to find me online. He lets his sleepy thoughts turn toward being with me. He is clearly letting me know he is thinking of me in new ways. We spar, my favorite thing to do. The words fly.

We go to a sexier place as we chat in the early morning. "What are you wearing?" he asks? Do I dare answer? Nothing very sexy I think but throw the query back to him. "What do you want me to be wearing?" I ask, buying time to think. "Pink silk," he answers immediately. "Then pink silk, it is," I say. "I look good in pink. It goes well with my white skin and dancing hazel eyes..." And so, we proceed to tease and taunt each other in a very suggestive way. We play for a while and then the workaholic in each of us kicks in and off we go to our respective jobs.

He and I often discuss business. We both come alive when there is a deal to make...perhaps we are kindred spirits despite the age difference. He is young and alive and has a great sense of humor. We laugh a lot when we talk, but where could we ever go regarding a relationship? He has started calling me "Hun" and loves it when he sees me online. He is very mysterious. When I ask if we can talk, he tells me not yet. That's interesting, but I understand if he wants to protect his identity. It's a smart move when you are online.

The General continues to send me emails. He is also softening. His term of endearment is "Dear." Glad neither of them uses the "Hey, Baby" line I so detest. I love the stability of the General. I sense that he will always be on a mission in life. I so hope I will have the power to really make him laugh and have some fun. I don't know how to live any other way, so having someone who will laugh and have fun with me is very important. Time will tell. I keep sending him happy stories and never remind him of where he is. He looks forward to our chats and my emails.

Mr. Bonsai is making small talk again. He never seems to want to meet or even talk on the phone, but he stops by in an email every day or sometimes twice a day. I certainly have the capacity to be a pen pal for a while more. I sense my life scares him a bit. I am forever on the go. I think he has a quiet, and perhaps more serene life.

Mr. Swift is still on the scene. He wants to know if I like taking vacations. He wants to go to LA and Ireland. He hasn't asked me, but always seems surprised when I answer his emails. He will send me some photos. At least he isn't so shy that he is afraid to correspond.

Ah, but I have been down this path before, all that assertiveness in the first email and then all I get is another pen pal! No one wants to go for coffee! Come on, you guys, why are you even on an online dating site? Dating! Don't you get it? Dating is a team sport; you simply can't do it alone.

Mr. Swift has sent me five emails today. He is finally telling me some things about himself and sends me his phone number. He tells me about his education and that he is retired. He never asks me for anything. That's good, Mr. Swift, keep it up, and please remember, no "hey, babies" allowed!

My thoughts turn to going on vacation with a stranger! Who would do that? I am back to watching Criminal Minds, so things like time alone and away with a complete stranger conjure up nothing but the most horrible images. It's truly a good thing you like to email, Mr. Swift, because I am so very far from going on vacation with you.

So is the man of my dreams really out there? Somehow, I thought I would at least get a few dates out of the dating service, and I guess I did: ten fantastic dates with Mr. Niceguy, but he was married. What's the deal? Do the married guys have more of a vested interest in dating than the single guys? The single guys seem to take so long, and in the end they never even ask for a date. The married guy turned out to be the kindest, gentlest, most compassionate, generous, and loving man who was unavailable! What's a girl to do? The complications are so difficult. I know I am taking the high road but taking it alone with such pain in my heart really doesn't feel very good. Oh well, tomorrow will be another day.

Chapter 20

FAMILY MEN

The morning started off with a chat with Baby Boy. He is softening in his words and asking more personal questions. Really wants more than that one great head shot of me. Will I send him photos? He still is not making moves to ask to meet me, yet he has started telling me where we will travel if he and I become a couple. I am confused about all this mystery. He is still calling me "Hun" and is expressing thoughts of compassion toward me. He gets into "helper" mode and wants to fix my life. It's nice to know those thoughts occur to him. He wants to know if I would take care of him, as well. He is a mystery, but that's part of his charm, I guess.

He is asking me to send him some photos of me. I ask "how?" He gives me his email address. That is a step I had not planned on, but I say "yes." Everything I know about him so far indicates that he is very well off. My vivid imagination goes to thoughts of this tall, handsome, impeccably dressed young man. How can I compete with that? If he sees my photos and doesn't like them, he can just slam the door on me and go back to his anonymity. It is very easy to disappear into the black hole of the virtual world. I worry that I won't be perfect enough for his elegant taste, although I have been known to turn a head or two in my own way. Since I heard the word "yes" come out of my mouth, or in this case, off my fingertips, I felt I had to follow through, so later that day I sent him my photos. There it was; the ball was in his court and I was holding my breath again. Why do I let myself fall into this situation over and over?

Mr. Niceguy pops onto IM to chat. He is broken-hearted. He misses me and wants to stay in touch. He wants to be friends…so do I. I hate that I have such strong feelings for him. I think about him all day and long for his touch. I will be strong, but none of this is making me very happy. We are both in pain. We chat for a while and then as the conversation starts to heat up a bit, I tell him I need to go to work. I probably should have told him I need a cold shower, but I didn't want to encourage that conversation.

Mr. Swift has emailed me seven times. He is pouring out his heart to me. He seems too excited. He sounds like he is ready to scoop me up and carry me away to some remote hut on a deserted island where we will live blissfully ever after! He needs to calm down, and I softly told him so. If he wants a relationship, we cannot start with being tied together. I haven't even seen his photo yet. I always get this Quasimodo image when I haven't seen a man's photo and he starts talking of love! It is so funny that I go there. I like his approach. He seems straightforward: divorced, lost a lot, but seems happy, loves his kids and grandkids. That is a selling point for me. Vacant dads make terrible husbands.

At some point when I start to care about a man, I like to ask him about his relationship with his own mom. A man who has a healthy relationship with his mom usually makes a better partner. He has a sense of family, of responsibility and of compassionate love. He is, unless he was very spoiled, usually less selfish. He has a sense of commitment to family. I like all of that.

In the evening I chat with Mr. Niceguy. We are so in love. He starts talking the "what about me" talk. Why should he stay in his marriage when he would be so happy with me? I stop that conversation right away. I remind him that he loves his kids and grandkids and that his wife has been a good woman towards him for a lot of years. He can't divorce his wife; it will change all of the relationships he holds precious. He and I can share the love of friendship…but nothing more. I tell him that if it is too hard for him to remain friends without a physical component, then I will go away forever. I see how hard this is on me as well as on him. I am not going to think about it too much. I need to see if we can have a controlled friendship or if we really have to part ways.

I won't have a physical relationship with a married man. My heart can't stand to be in that situation, and I want to maintain my dignity. Throwing away your moral values messes with your head. I can be strong, and I am smart enough to walk away if I see myself getting weak.

At 2 am the General comes online. He is calling me "dear" and "my love." He is starting to talk about our relationship and buying a new house where we will live. I tell him I am not ready to talk about such things. I need to get to know him face-to-face. I need to know we are compatible. We get into an interesting discussion about physical relationships. With him discussions about physical love are not about sex; at least not in the way those discussions are with other men. He is serious, never playful. He keeps going back to talking about inner beauty and how important that is. Is he trying to tell me he isn't really attracted to my body? Is he more turned on by my mind and my soul? Well, I can tell you that if the body part of the relationship is missing from the mind- body-soul, then I am not interested! Been there, done that, don't want that again. The guy that wins my heart is going to know how to rock my world physically. Balance is everything in life and you realize that most when you have had none!

The General and I talk until 4 am. It has been the longest conversation and the deepest ever. He will be home in two months, and we will meet then. He asked me if we could write a book together. Ah, so you do know how to soften me, don't you, General? I am excited to think about all I can learn from him. He has seen the most horrific side of human beings. The side that can kill for no reason other than they have been told to. Putting aside all political views, I am amazed that it is humanly possible to kill another person, not out of some raging temper, but out of allegiance to some political entity! The thought makes me shudder. I am the first one to show my appreciation for anyone in the American military system who is protecting me and my fellow Americans, but it is so hard to think of why that is a necessary evil.

My thoughts turn to the General and how I pray for his safety every day. I also pray that he hasn't been too tainted by his military existence. Will he be able to look at things in a soft, compassionate way, or will his entire life remain a mission of protecting us from all evil? This remains to be seen. As much as I like the General, I think there is so much to him that is still hidden. It has been his job for over thirty years to serve in the military. He has been in charge of the most difficult missions in war-torn areas of the world. He has had to watch his back and the backs of his troops for years. Will he ever be off guard? Will he always be at-the-ready whenever we are together?

He hasn't been with a woman in a very long time. I worry that all he has seen and experienced will get in the way of our having a real relationship, one with spontaneity, passion, sensuality and all the tenderness needed for me to stay with this man. The mechanics of operating a relationship are not very attractive to me. I guess it's his stiff way of writing that worries me. I love to laugh, and no matter what I do, I don't sense that he is able. That might not be completely fair, since he is in the middle of a peace-keeping mission overseas, but I feel I am really trying to lighten his day with my emails and

IM chats to help him feel that there is hope waiting for him. I worry that he will build up our relationship in his mind and when he comes home, I might not like him at all. He would be crushed, and I would feel so horrible.

This virtual dating is fraught with all sorts of problems. How do you get to know someone without meeting them, wait an "appropriate" amount of time, make plans to meet them, and find you were so far off base? I often like what these men are saying and how they tell me they will behave, but it is truly just smoke and mirrors. So little of it is real. You can't tell from a thumbnail photo all you need to know about a person's physical attributes any more than you can tell from a few emails that you are compatible.

Here I am, looking for that mind-body-soul connection, but who am I kidding? Do I expect to have even a glimmer of hope from this online model? Here I am, seventeen days into this forum and I have been called names, dumped by email, and fallen in love, only to have to give that up! What a roller coaster ride! Where do I really stand?

Mr. Niceguy would run to my side in a heartbeat, and except for the small problem of his wife, I would gladly take him in.

Baby Boy loves to talk – several times a day. He says really nice things, but he has not made even the slightest move toward wanting to make a date to meet me.

Mr. Bonsai is truly a pen pal. Several times a day he checks in, gives me a weather report, and checks out. He loves music and is always going to some sort of concert. I would go to a concert, if only he would ask.

Mr. Swift sounds great, but a bit too ready to make a move, at least on paper. No talk of dating yet, but I think it's because he is respecting the fact that I gave him a schedule to follow!

Then there is the occasional sighting of the gopher-men who pop their heads out of the gopher holes, say, "look at me," and then retreat! They confuse me. Do they look at my profile, decide to give it a try and, when I reply, get too scared to follow through? Is that how they do everything in life? I start to think about how much fun it would be to interview them. Could I get a real glimpse into how they view this process or why they run for the hills when a woman they chose to contact says hello? I think it's more sad than funny. Maybe there should be a rules and regulations guide to better help them follow this process. After seventeen days, although I have gone on ten dates with a wonderful married man, I am not much better off. I still do not have a man in my life to get to know and love. I will say this though: I am starting to feel more like a woman, but some days it's more like a rejected woman!

Chapter 21

UNCOVERING TRAITS

The morning starts with an IM chat with Baby Boy. I am thrilled! He loves my photos and says I look so beautiful in the cobalt blue outfit I had on in one of them. I can't believe he is even still talking with me! I seem to have such an inferiority complex around him. His words are sweet and sexy. He loves waking up and talking with me before he gets out of bed. He always asks where I am and what I'm wearing. Some days I think my playfulness takes over and I tell him exactly what he wants to hear! We spar. We banter. We get each other excited.

He finally knows my name and has begun using it when he writes to me. I still do not know his! I am a bit frustrated by all of that, and my vivid mind starts to wander. What if he is really famous? What if he is handsome? What if he really chooses me? It's a fun dream and I know that no harm is done by my dreaming it. He may never make a move, though he often asks what I would do living the high life. He is always jetting off somewhere, or is he? Is he just a lonely guy with an imagination more vivid than mine? He is such fun that I don't mind. Whether his life is really fabulous, or he works the third shift in some shop somewhere, I don't care. I love the way he banters with words and paints a beautiful fairy-tale life. He is clearly an intellectual match for me, and that's been so much fun.

We laugh a lot when we banter. We type very fast and keep the quips coming for hours. I love waking up to him in the virtual world, and whether I ever wake up to him in real life, he has been a fun partner. Today was a bit different though. Perhaps because I had sent him photos and really felt he would reject me, I feel excited. He, too, seems more excited to be playing our morning game. Words come fast and easy today. We get into the "sex" talk immediately! Things heat up much faster to that crescendo and then the climax. Whew! That was easy!

I laugh when he tells me he needs to go back to sleep! Is this going to be your pattern, Baby Boy? Will you always roll over to sleep when I want to snuggle? I need to find out more about him and his habits, or do I dare? It has been days since I've even remembered our age difference. I have let the reality of all that slip into the shadows of our time online together. He's young and smart and oh such fun. As long as we have no plans to meet, I can create any reality I want. I can become his age or he mine. We can fall madly in love or just remain friends. He can escape into the great abyss of virtual suspense where one never knows if the other will ever respond. I am choosing to have this fling and play the sex kitten each morning. I know I stand a chance of never meeting him because we have shared so much, but I don't think I will mind whatever comes next. Baby Boy has been a blast to play with.

Well, I must have written down the wrong phone number for Mr. Swift. I called the number I had, and it was wrong. I feel bad since I imagine he will feel that I have stood him up. I will email an apology to him later. I think I would like to meet him. At least he seems real. He claims to be divorced and seems to be intelligent. There is no harm in getting to know him.

Mr. Niceguy and I talked on the phone. He misses me, as I do him. We talk a bit and, when we are ready to hang up, he says, "I love you." I try to stay upbeat and tell him I love him, too.

I need a break from all this, and it's only been eighteen days! I think I'll take a walk and stay away from my computer for a while today. I need to clear my head.

Later in the day, I finally connect by phone with Mr. Swift. He doesn't sound at all like I envisioned. He almost has a whiney quality to his voice. I think he feels bad that he had given me the wrong number. I don't mind; at least we have connected. We talk for a while. He tells me a bit about his life and his past. He seems nice enough. We will see if he ever sends me photos. I know he wants to meet me, but not yet. I want to see what he looks like first.

The General has been very quiet since our long talk. I don't know if he is just busy or if he was upset by all the talk about mind-body-soul connections. We will see if he has vanished or not. Time will tell, and, after more than 40 emails and many chats, he too will probably just go into the great abyss of online rejections. It can really be a cruel world.

Got a quick note from Mr. Smoker. He says that he sees from my profile that I will not go out with a smoker. I am in a playful mood, so I say, "Oh, don't go away mad. I'm just allergic to smoke, not to nice men." He writes back that he is interested in me. I do the lowest thing and simply don't answer. I know it's unfair and it is the thing I hate the most when it's done to me, but today, I simply don't have the energy. Sorry, Mr. Smoker, I should have been nicer.

Got another note from a very nice man who tells me that he is not a professional and would probably never have a chance with me, but he is a nice man and would like to get to know me. I feel sorry for him and feel like my profile makes me out to be a snob since it says I am looking for a professional businessman. I write a nice note back. He replies, but who knows whether or not it will continue.

In the evening, Mr. Niceguy chats with me and does a video call. My heart breaks. I can hardly talk with him. I want to be in his arms. He tells me he can't stand being without me. This is so hard. I get the image of a man in prison behind the bulletproof shield, putting his hand against the glass, and his woman reaching out and touching the glass in return. I know I am not ready to see him, so I try to cut the conversation off as soon as possible. I am sad. He is sad, too.

Chapter 22

MAKING MONEY

This morning I have several emails waiting for me from Baby Boy, Mr. Swift, Mr. Bonsai and a few new men who "are interested in me"! Baby Boy is happy I have sent more photos, and he tells me how beautiful I am. He wishes he were with me. He wants to kiss me. Really? Funny, I haven't caught your name yet! I think the suspense is getting to me. Don't any of the single men ever make a move?????

I promised myself thirty days of online dating – no more. I am already at nineteen days and have only had some dates from a married man. I would say I am not doing well at all. I have lots of pen pals and one married friend who would fly to my side if I allowed. This is pathetic.

Mr. Swift sends me email after email. I wonder if he will ever send me a photo or ask me out for coffee. He really sounds interested, but I am being cautious after my bad experience with Mr. Lack of Technology.

I scratch my head and wonder why men pay money to join a dating site and then simply become pen pals for a while. I must be sending out negative vibes.

Mr. Niceguy chats with me. We try being cordial without going down the road to romance. I sense the tenseness between us, but we have lots to say to each other and none of it is overly romantic. We are friends and I see that we each genuinely care about each other. I think that knowing he loves me and knowing he will respect me gives me a sense of peace and belonging, even if we can't see each other. We talk for hours.

The General has been painfully quiet. I haven't heard from him in two days. Knowing where he is, I am always worried about his safety. It is his safety rather than the thought that he has stopped liking me that worries me. I just have to wait. I really have no choice in the matter at all. He is a very respectful man and I hope that, even if he has lost interest in me, he will write to tell me goodbye. Time will tell. I send him a cute photo of me to see if that gets him to write.

Baby Boy loves getting emails from me. He always amazes me with his sweet comments. I call him my pen pal. I don't know if he will like it or if it will make him upset since he is saying such sweet things. I still think he is sending me mixed messages. Maybe he is creating that aura of suspense on purpose. I feel guarded. I just don't know where this is going.

Mr. Swift continues to send me loving notes. He seems so excited every time I answer an email! I get the sense he feels like a cat that has caught the canary. Not so fast, Mr. Swift. I haven't even seen your face. I wonder if you will be the next one to make a move. After all, you have sent me so many emails and have made so many hints about how excited you are to be getting to know me. We'll see.

It is almost comical how this forum can bring such highs and lows across the emotional spectrum. A man sends a flirt, so you read his profile. If you like what you read, you can flirt back or even take the time to email him. Then you can email back and forth for days before he drops off the face of the planet. I think the system simply needs to be changed! Why, even the cavemen had better dating skills. They saw a woman they wanted, hit her over the head, dragged her off and they mated. Short, sweet (or maybe not) and to the point! Come on fellas, what's a girl got to do to meet for coffee?

81

Chapter 23

REEVALUATING THE ACTION

Well, there are all sorts of kids in the dating pool today. Lots of new emails from men all over the country. Wonder what I did to inspire this! We'll see who really comes out to play in a few days. We now have Texas, Virginia, Maine and Minnesota all in the running. My email count is well over 300 emails in twenty days! I am beginning to think I should run for political office. I think I would win the votes of all the men. I am very tempted here to write the acronym "LOL" that one uses to tell you they have made a funny point in the conversation, just in case you are too stupid or dense to get it.

It is an interesting online world and a good deal of it goes completely over my baby boomer head. I always thought I had a great sense of humor and have gotten through 63 years on this planet never having to have someone tap me on the shoulder to tell me they were making a joke. Now that I am in this cold, virtual world, I guess I need to be told whether something is funny or not. The sad thing is that often what I feel would truly be considered insults in the face-to-face world are considered "laugh out loud" funny statements in the virtual world! Go figure!

Well, there are several emails from Mr. Bonsai this morning. He has finally sent me his photo. I am glad since I hate communicating with a faceless being. He looks like a pleasant guy and has now taken to emailing me fifteen times a day. He loves music and, what do you know, he says we should try dancing sometime! Good move, Mr. Bonsai. I would like that. We'll see how long it takes for you to actually ask me out. You aren't softening in terms of calling me any names of endearment. You seem to simply like corresponding with me. I am fine with that. You have at least started to tell me a bit about your life.

Mr. Swift is starting to get excited about our correspondence. He tells me lots about himself, and with every email he tells me he is interested in me and that I make him happy. He has sent me photos and hopes I like them. Again, he is a nice guy who hasn't made a move. I am never going to get over the fact that the only one who has asked me out is the one married man.

The General is back. His notes are usually the same. I just don't have much sense about his personality. I suppose he knows that he is in a difficult situation and won't be in the states for a while, so he doesn't want to get my hopes up. I hope he won't be hurt if and when I see him. I am not sure my ever-ready bunny personality and his straightforward attitude will ever be a good match. I am just going to let this one ride. I cannot predict where this is going. For now, I continue to write to him to cheer him up.

Baby Boy and I chatted for a long while this morning. I love when we really talk. It's fun and intellectually stimulating. He can be serious one minute and then get suggestive the next. He absolutely loves my photos. He's so cute when he tells me how beautiful I am. He will be chatting for a while and then suddenly say, "I can't stop looking at your picture." So endearing! Lately he has been talking about when we are together and how much fun it will be. He has even started asking what my favorite color is. "Why?" I ask. "I need to know so that I can buy you a present." "No presents," I say. When he talks about being together, I ask how I will know what he looks like. He laughs and tells me I will know and I don't have to worry; I will like what I see. I laugh and try to hint at how unfair it is that I don't know what he looks like. He simply shrugs it off. I call him Mystery Man. I know that he has the upper hand, so I back down. He has really softened up and I enjoy talking with him. He is smart and funny with a hint of being a really sensual guy. Who wouldn't like that? I simply keep trying to forget that none of the single guys ever seem to want to make the first move. It is almost comical at this point.

Before I go to sleep, I have received a few emails from Mr. Swift, Mr. Bonsai and Baby Boy. I get excited to see whether they will make a move. I have less than ten days and then I will no longer exist to this audience. As each day unfolds, I am in amazement that so much "virtual" activity has taken place. I just wanted to go on a few dates!

Mr. Niceguy tells me how beautiful I look and how much he loves and misses me. I miss you, too, my dear, but rules are rules. I know that I can't see you and maintain my composure. I would give anything to have your arms wrapped tightly around me in a locked-lip kiss. I long for your touch and the tenderness with which you touch me. I long for your tongue tracing circles in my ear and down my neck until your soft, supple lips are sweetly planted on my mouth. How did I ever let this happen, and more importantly, will I ever feel this again with anyone? Anyone?

Chapter 24

WADING THROUGH THE MUCK

I have found that there is a trick to finding new men to correspond with instantly. I log into the chat room and just stay there a while. I never say anything because as an old boomer, I haven't a clue what's going on or what they are saying! By just hanging out, men take notice and send me an instant message. Usually, they are at least 15 years younger than I am (bless my photographer!), so there isn't much to say. Sometimes I simply tell them they are too young, or I say if they don't have a photo, I won't talk with them.

I love to read a profile. You get a glimpse into how they think. Today is no exception. Hung out in the chat room for a bit and got six new messages. A 34-year-old, a 47-year-old, and several others. No real need to chat with them, but it was fine.

Mr. Philly is starting to chat with me. Mr. Swift is already missing me since he knows I will be off the site in a few days. I thought I would surprise him with a phone call, but only got a voice message. He will be shocked when he sees that I've called. He is really starting to like me. I think I may want to meet him. He would love that.

Mr. Bonsai loves music and has sent me many videos. I can just imagine him dancing around the room with arms flailing but having a great time. Maybe now that he is emailing me so many times a day, he will eventually ask me out. He has finally sent me his photo. One is a sweet one with him holding his baby granddaughter. He's got a brain and a love of music and fun. I wouldn't mind going out with him to see if we actually connect.

The General finally wrote me a long email. He says he is serious about starting a relationship with me. My response is that whether we ever date or not, I hope we will stay friends. I think we will have fun writing a book together. The more he writes to me, the more I am softening. I wonder if he will. I have a feeling that he is the kind of guy who, if he loves a woman, will be everything to her. She would not be disappointed, but to the outside world, he would never show it. He would remain calm and composed. His emails deepen. He looks for my emails and wishes he could write more often. He loves knowing what I am doing. He has finally revealed his entire name to me. I must admit, I am dreaming of the day I meet him. It is such a wonderful moment in my head.

I spoke with Mr. Swift on the phone. I think I like his words rather than his voice. He clearly wants to meet me. I don't know yet. He seems depressed, even though he writes in a very positive way. I am getting mixed signals from him.

Mr. Bonsai sends me email after email. He never commits. He talks of his family and sends me funny jokes and videos. He seems very easygoing. I enjoy writing to him. He is smart, and I know that he loves music. I could just have some fun with him if he asked me out. He has relaxed. He tells me about his family.

I love when men love their children and grandchildren. It makes me think that they will make better partners in a relationship. I always look for their hearts to show. Guys who are online only for sex don't ever show that side of themselves. They are focused on wooing you in some fashion. We have already established that there are the "Hey, Baby" guys, the poetic "I'll relocate for you" guys, and the lonely guys.

Every once in a while, you will meet the real guys who live with the hope that they will find a woman to love even in this skewed and distorted forum. Often, they have loved before and remember the good times, the feelings of warmth and belonging, the close bonds, both physical and emotional, that come with having a good woman by their side. Yes, those guys are online, too, but you do have to wade through a lot of muck to find them.

On my worst days, I can call a spade a spade and write someone off with a cryptic email around honesty or the lack thereof. On my better days, I do take the time to open the lines of communication to see if they will reveal their true selves. You still have to take everything with a grain of salt since some guys are so skillful at bending the truth.

There is a new man on this scene, Mr. Tennessee. Handsome and smart. Unfortunately, I was not having one of my better days when he first emailed me, and I think I left him cold. I was simply brutal in my comments. I should have waited to email him at a time when I wasn't so tired of this whole online scene. Oh well, we'll see if he ever writes back. I laugh at how easy it is to make or break your chances of getting to know someone. My rule is never to chase. I will not pursue him. He wrote to me, I answered, he rebutted, and I went in for the kill. Too bad. We will see if he decides to try again. I don't know why he would, but maybe he will sense that there is some good in me, even on my off days!

I send out emails to Baby Boy and the General before I go to sleep. Both men are softening, and I am interested in each in a different way. The General would provide complete stability, but the decision is out as to whether or not he will light my fire. Baby Boy could light my fire with a word or glance, but would I always be wondering when he was going to drop me for a younger woman?

Mr. Niceguy and Mr. Bonsai both send me emails before I go to sleep. Mr. Niceguy is really missing me, and although I hate to admit it, I miss him terribly. Remember, he was my first and only online date. He lit me up and showed me that I could be a real woman again. It was wonderful. His wife is the dilemma. I haven't seen him, and hope I won't cave, but I have doubts about my strength. Mr. Bonsai is fun to chat with. He is so light-hearted. No pressure of any kind. He sends me funny videos and cartoons. He has a great sense of humor.

Chapter 25

ASSESSING THE RELATIONSHIPS

Mr. Bonsai is up early and emailing me. He seems to have become a constant. He makes me laugh.

There is also a reply from Baby Boy to my late-night email. He reminds me that he is looking for love, not just friendship with me. I am not going there yet. He still needs to feel comfortable talking with me on the phone and meeting me. I can take it slowly. He loves the letter I sent him. He compliments my writing ability. He briefly makes promises that hint at "soon," but I wonder if he will call or invite me to meet. I always have my doubts about him and this relationship. He is so young.

Mr. Bonsai sends me so many emails today. He just talks and asks questions. He sends me jokes and funny videos. I feel like we can talk, but I have no clue as to whether he would ever ask me out. No matter, he is smart, and I can at least enjoy our email exchanges. He even throws in a compliment occasionally.

I've had quite a few new emails today. I won't reply to most, but I got a beautiful note from Mr. Dad, who seems nice. He seems sincere without all of that pent-up sexual frustration that I sense in some. We will exchange emails and see where it goes. He has two kids, but I don't know how old. I think they must be fairly grown since he told me his son picked my photo out and said to write me! Think about it: we now live in a world where our kids can pick people of the opposite sex for us to date!

I suddenly don't feel so great. I have been in a line-up for nearly a month. Men can ogle my photo and try to get me to write. I had a few exchanges with a man, but I must have had a flash of meanness in me, since the man smoked, and I told him I didn't even want to write to him because of the smoking. There was really no reason to do that. We were only talking! I am becoming warped.

Baby Boy comes on IM to chat. I did not expect him to chat in the afternoon. He talks for a while. I take one of his jokes the wrong way and go cold. I don't want to talk, and I tell him I have to go. He pursues me and asks if he did something to offend me. I tell him yes, and what hurt so much. We talk a bit more, much sweeter this time. He tells me he is getting horny. "I can't help," I say. "If we were talking on the phone, I could help you out." He laughs! I have to go, so I just leave.

Mr. Tennessee comes back with a vengeance! This time both he and his daughter will relocate for me! "Slow down," I say. I insist he stops this nonsense; I really can't stand it. I think he will be back tomorrow!

Chapter 26

RED FLAGS

Woke up much too early. Baby Boy was online. "Up early," I said. He tells me that he wanted to talk with me, so he got up. We start to chat and can't seem to stop. We are going deeper and talk about so many personal things. He starts to reveal more and more about himself. Not too much flirting; this is serious business, and he wants to tell me his story. He really trusts me now, but he is afraid that I will stop caring about him if he tells me the truth. In a way, he is right.

What he reveals is so difficult to hear. I feel betrayed and confused. I get a horrible feeling in the pit of my stomach. How could I ever go out with this man? His secret is safe with me (no, I am not going to reveal it to you), but I know that life together would be so hard. I think both he and I would be on the fringe of society as a couple. There would be so many taboos that we would forget which one was most prominent on any given day.

Suddenly, he calls me on the phone! He has a sexy voice, and we talk for a short while. I am shocked but glad. I had no audio or visual of him before, so I am glad to at least hear his voice. We don't talk long. I think he was just trying to make the point that he is still in control. He calls whenever he wants to. I am so confused. I feel that he is a person who really needs a friend right now, and I don't want to abandon him as he goes through many things, really tough things. I know my personality, and I will remain his friend, but the more I know about him, the more I know he is in for a very bumpy ride.

Well, there are some new men on the horizon. Mr. Tennessee is back with a vengeance and Mr. Dad is also trying hard to get my attention. Somehow, all that sweet talk just creeps me out! I am into reality, not false compliments. The newest group of men has moved from "Hey, Baby" to "Sweetie" and "Honey." I always have my guard up! The more I know about myself, the more I see that I am turned on by intelligence. Give me a great sparring partner any day! I miss Mr. Lack of Technology!

Baby Boy is back online in the evening. He spends lots of time chatting with me. He seems relieved that I have not run away. I know his deepest secret and still haven't run for the hills. I sent him another photo of me. To my amazement, he tells me he has printed it out! He is very appreciative of the woman I am.

Mr. Bonsai is my favorite pen pal. He writes at least five times a day. He has turned into a pretty good replacement for Mr. Lack of Technology, but I still miss that guy.

Mr. Bonsai is fun. I like his style and the fact that so much of his life is about music. Mr. Bonsai and I discuss how he has a "harem" of women to go out with. Somehow men seem to be better (and less criticized) for that lifestyle than women. I have had emails from men who ask me to stop emailing all other men as soon as they send their first "hello." They want exclusivity and haven't even heard my voice. It always amazes me. It is really a catch 22: if I try to develop a platonic relationship with more than one man, I feel like I am cheating on the other. I have to watch that my heart doesn't get in the way. I find that when I email a man a few times he starts to get into that "ownership" mindset.

I currently email a few men whom I have never met, and some are starting to send me "We will live happily ever after" emails. They do things like send me contracts that they have procured granting them lots of money, so I will know they are financially stable. It is interesting really, and sad. The other thing that is sad is that I have gotten over 325 emails from men over this past month, and only two have asked me out. I have lots of great pen pals, for which I am grateful, but I wonder why men go onto an online dating site if they don't want to date. Some want to talk sex because they feel secure in the anonymity of the online world. Others know they don't want to date and really do just need the diversion of writing to a woman. The married guys don't waste a minute. They want to date and plan to, if only there was a way to hide that wife!

Chapter 27

AT WHAT POINT IS IT CHEATING?

Every day starts with Baby Boy; we talk for hours. He likes to play and joke and he gets really serious when we talk about what will come next in his life. I think he is starting to rely on my wisdom and my openness. I don't back down when he talks about his problems. He is getting very close to me.

There are a few new men on the scene, Mr. Marketing. Really smart and very professional. I wasn't going to write to him because he smokes, but he pursued. He immediately asked for my email address. He sends me great one-liners. How I love a man who spars! We keep each other in stitches. He says, "This is a test to see if my email gets to you, even if I don't." I reply, "It has happily gotten to me, and maybe you will, too!" He replies, "Now that sounds like a plan!" I reply, "A one-liner??? Aren't you the Marketing guy? You are supposed to say, 'but wait there's more!'" He replies, "Well, I certainly hope there is more and if you order now you get his-and-hers watches." I say, "Now, that's the spirit! Only $19.95, right?" He says, "All I need is conversation with you and a coffee, and I am good to go." You see, it doesn't take much to get me interested: a quick banter and some hint of a plan to meet. It would be fun.

Let's see if Mr. Marketing is a mover and shaker. Well, Mr. BrownEyes certainly is! He sent me an email, asked for my number, called me and made a date! Listen up you guys who have been on dating sites for years. That's how it's done! He wants to meet for coffee. After some thought, he decides that wine and appetizers would be much more fun. I agree. So, after 325 emails from all sorts of men, I finally have man number 2 asking me out. I am already planning what to wear and thinking I need to remember to shave my legs...that is a very forward thought for me. What on earth do I have in mind?

The day progresses with Mr. Dad trying desperately to reach me, and I wasn't available most of the day to talk. I promise him that we can chat at 11 pm. I know without knowing him that he will be waiting all night to chat. I keep my promise and we chat for a while, and then he asks if we can talk on the phone. I seem to attract men who have strong accents. He has a very strong Irish accent. I am surprised by that, but we chat for a while and then I try to go off to bed.

Just as I am ready to fall asleep, a new man arrives on the scene, Mr. Construction. He and I chat on IM and then on the phone. Guess what! He has a very strong German accent! I can hardly understand him. I ask him to send photos. When they arrive, I am not very excited. Now what? How do I let him off easy? I hate being mean. I hate slamming the virtual door on another person. I will have to think about this. The night becomes full of demons. I absolutely cannot sleep! Too much activity!

Am I cheating on each of these men by writing to the other? How do I know whom to go out with when I haven't met any of them? I toss and turn. I am sleepless. I know exactly what I need to relieve all of this tension, but I have no one to help me with that!

Chapter 28

SMOKING – THE ULTIMATE DEAL BREAKER

I wake up with the mood of the century! I am having one royal pity party! The lack of sleep, the lack of human touch, the lack of the presence of testosterone in my life is taking its toll. To top it off, it is a grey and rainy day. Disaster! Baby Boy sees that I am online. He asks how I am, and I let go. He thought he was the one in a bad mood, but I played "Can you top this?" with him. No matter what he said, I countered with a negative. It was the kind of day where I could not get out of my own way! I was so miserable. I told him that our relationship wasn't working for me. I needed a man that I could be with and count on, not this figment of my imagination.

He is defensive and reminds me of how close we've grown and how sweet and kind his words are to me. I counter that they are just words. I spent my entire life with a man who was no more than words…no actions. I was tired of all that! I needed a real man. I kept being mean throughout his trying to tell me jokes and trying to turn me on. He was desperate. Finally, he simply gave up and said goodbye.

Mr. Dad is now sending me proof that he will be out of the country on a work assignment for three weeks. I think with the time difference, I will be able to relax a bit. He wants my phone number so we can text. He sends me a copy of his plane ticket. He is trying too hard. I don't know yet how I feel about him. I really don't like intense; I am intense enough for two people!

Mr. Construction tries to IM me several times. I ignore him because I am working, and I really don't know what to say. This is hard. I don't get the impression that he will be the kind of man who will take no for an answer!

Mr. Bonsai continues to delight me with his humor and constant emails. He's a good pen pal and I hope that one day I will get to meet him.

And new on the scene is Mr. Steamy (hey, if Grey's Anatomy can have one, so can I!). He is so cute. Wow! If he sent me his real photo, then count me in. The only problem I see is that he, too, has sent me the same email with the 23 questions and pretty much the same answers as several other men. Honestly, they make me feel like I am getting senile. I have read the same thing over and over. If one more man likes Malaysian Pizza, I will scream. What on earth is it anyway? I email back and am a bit cryptic at the beginning but soften toward the end of the email. I am hoping that he writes back, but my fangs were out, so who knows. He, like many of the men, is a widower and has one child he is raising. His daughter is also beautiful. I sincerely hope that neither will relocate for me. The collection of the "fast and furious" is still growing. Mr. Steamy will be a thing of the past right away.

In the afternoon, Baby Boy comes on IM to chat. He asks if I am still in a mood. "Of course not," I say. "I keep my pity parties short." I hate pity, especially if it is self-inflicted. He gives me a "brb," the acronym for be right back, and suddenly he is calling my cell phone. He decided I needed to hear his voice. He wants me to know how beautiful, kind and gorgeous I am. He is trying so hard to make me feel better. I appreciate that. He tells me funny stories, and I tell him a joke. We put each other in a much better mood.

Before he gets off the phone, he lays another bomb on me!
He is a smoker. When was he going to tell me that! That is a
deal breaker! I hate smoke and have no desire to kiss a mouth
that tastes like cigarettes! Shall I tell him tomorrow? We'll see
how I feel.

Mr. Dad comes on IM. It seems he is headed to New York to fly to the Pacific for a three-week contract. We talk a bit and then I read the words as I type, "I don't live far from New York!" What am I thinking! I am inviting him to meet me. Let me tell you, he is all over that! "Great, I will call you as soon as I arrive, and we can set a place to meet." I tell him there is a great restaurant halfway between us, and he is ready.

There is a knot in the pit of my stomach. Why do I feel like this? Oh well, it's only lunch and then he will be off for three weeks, and who knows, I might like him. We make all the arrangements, chat some more and then he calls me. "I want to hear your voice and say 'sweet dreams'." A nice end to the evening, or so I thought.

I check my email once more before retiring. There are a few from Mr. Bonsai. We send emails back for a while. He sends me music to listen to, and our conversation starts to get a bit racy for the first time ever. I am surprised, but on some level pleased because I have been talking to him as if we have been friends for a very long time. He tells me when he has dates and so do I. We talk about all sorts of things and I, the naïve thing that I am, always see the platonic. I guess I was wrong. I think he is just a cautious guy who wants to get to know someone first. That's just plain smart. We have already established a trusting relationship, and now he is showing interest. I like that. He always has music in his heart...not a bad quality.

Mr. Niceguy is still emailing me and calling me. We are tied at the heart. I miss him so much and he misses me. I can't see him. He knows, but he will forever try to convince me that we can be just friends. I know we can't.

There is such a passion between us. I am electrified whenever I see him, and he just wants to touch me. He strokes my face and pulls me close to kiss me. His arms are always around me when we are together. I needed to stop that before I did something I would forever regret. The bond of marriage has always been sacred to me.

I need to be strong and not minimize my principles. This is very hard because I am just waking up as a woman. Sheer conflict. I know that I need to take the high road, and I also know that he has been such a good advisor to me, such a good confidant, such a good and tender lover, how can I resist the temptation to simply be with him. I really want to see him but know that this time it would not be as platonic as before, and so I resist.

Chapter 29

SELF-WORTH –
HOW DO YOU GET YOURS?

I woke up very early this morning. All that hot talk last night with Mr. Bonsai. The music he sent put me right to sleep, and so getting to bed earlier caused me to wake up earlier. A beautiful letter from the General was waiting. He is so deep and so tender. Every word tells a story. Every word makes me melt. I long to meet him. I long to hear and know him. I long to feel his arms around me. I am comforted just by reading his emails. He makes me feel safe. We have already exchanged more than 60 emails, and things have really turned the corner. We are connected now in a way that I do not feel with anyone else. He is never throwing out sexual innuendos. He is a gentleman always, yet he exudes love and tenderness.

It is hard to describe how I feel. I don't know whether it is partly the concept of what he does, what he stands for, or what he says, but I know that if it is possible to love someone you have never met, then I am in love. I care so deeply for this man whose spirit is so beautiful. I don't get the idea that he is just copying words from some loveguru.com website like the others. I feel he is honest, and his words are his own. I have even tried to search for quotes using pieces of his emails to see if he, like so many of the others, is simply copying from some site. I can find no similarities.

There is also a quick note from Mr. BrownEyes and five from Mr. Bonsai.

Just as I thought, our first ever spicy exchange last night made him sleepless. Still up at 2 am, he was thinking of me and sending me music. This morning I write to say I thought our conversation might have had a sleepless effect on him. I know that I will hear from him when he wakes.

There is some heat coming from Mr. Dad. He is convinced that he needs a good woman, and I am it! He is like a caveman, and I am expecting the club at any moment! I am uneasy, but he tells me he is coming to New York before he travels to Malaysia and wants to meet me. I make plans, but he stands me up! He is off the next day and demands that I call and text him. He calls me at all hours and is unhappy if I do not respond. The relationship feels abusive… it's not for me, but how do I tell him? Well, I have to see how brave I am.

Every day there is a new collection of emails and flirts from guys, some interesting and some not, but I am completely amazed that after all this time, I am still getting the volume of emails that I did earlier. Was it something I said or simply that great head shot of me? I like the attention, but of course, so much of it is false. The lies abound with man after man sending me photos of gorgeous guys (not of themselves), all who have lost wives and all who have beautiful daughters!

The trouble is that I am so tired of the lies that I have stopped being nice. I simply send them the email I have received, which is a duplicate of their own, and ask if it doesn't look painfully suspicious! Once I start writing to them, where will the scam come in? If it all starts with a lie, what will come next? It is really tiring and wrong on many levels. I have spent my life doing good, helping others, making a difference, and I guess for that reason, I am a prime target for the liars of the world. I always think people are telling the truth. What reason would they have to lie? The online dating experience has proven me wrong. Men love to lie, especially when they feel protected. Luckily, I have, so far, not fallen too far into the lies and have been able to protect myself and my property. I am much more cautious and aware than

I ever was in the past. I hope that I will always stay sharp and not make a horrible mistake.

So today is like the rest; I have my favorites who write to me: Mr. Niceguy, Mr. Bonsai, the General, Baby Boy and now Mr. BrownEyes and Mr. Marketing Man. No dates since I decided not to see Mr. Niceguy, but lots of great emails and IM conversations. Occasionally, Mr. 45 pops back into my life to play, but that is a rare occurrence and only for a bit of online flirting. We sometimes talk about the whole online experience and trade stories. Most of the stories are sad and unfruitful…and yet we stay connected!

Baby Boy is changing his tune. He really wants to meet me, but when he asks if I have a couch in my office, I know what kind of "meeting" he wants to have. No, that's not going to happen. There were things before that would prevent me from seeing him, but his latest revelations, coupled with the fact that he now tells me he smokes, has cooled any romantic feelings I might have had. We can talk as friends.

Mr. Niceguy sends me a text: "I wish you were in my arms." I melt and call him. He has such a pull to my heart. I love hearing his voice. I love the things he says to me and how worried he is about me. I love that he feels I am a completely different woman than I was when we met, and he is right. I am clearly happier, wiser and more confident that there will be someone out there for me.

Lies or not, I have heard many men tell me how beautiful I am, and it feels good. I needed to hear it so that I could raise my level of self-worth. I didn't realize how painfully little I had.

The General continues to amaze me. His letters are filled with love. He is so poetic and yet so strong. I am falling hard, and I have never laid eyes on the man. He tells me that with every beat of his heart, he is mine and asks me to take care of his heart because I own it now. He tells me that I only need to look to the stars to know how vast his love is for me. He NEVER talks about sex. Previously, all my emails in response to his have been very cautious and reserved. I send him hugs for safety, but never profess my love.

Recently, I have thrown caution to the wind and have started telling him what traits I see in him that I love and respect. I want to scream, "Just get home so we can be together!" I know better. I know that we can be anything online so there is no guarantee that he is even in the Army in Iraq or holds any official position. I want to believe that he is above lying, but I know that I cannot trust that. I just have to wait and protect my heart, but I really want to be wrapped in his arms. I am often sleepless as my fantasies take over and I dream of mad, passionate nights with this amazing man!

I am always amazed at how easy it has been for me to fall into the trap of thinking that I know someone simply from their emails. I am a writer and truly love words. Don't I realize that any man with the least bit of skill could pen a note that would break my heart or take me places filled with fantasy? How could I, a lover of the written word, be so foolish as to think that their notes are true?

The General has an amazing gift with words. He writes of the most tender things. He stays in character, never slipping into the "fast and furious" lure of sex with a stranger. He makes me feel that he would always see me with his heart before he ever saw me with his eyes. I am falling so deeply in love with the image of him. Time will tell; he should be home in six weeks. Of course, by then I may be a lost cause! I am already worried about my heart. I think of him morning, noon and night. I lose sleep dreaming of him and how wonderful it will be to build a life with him. Again, all this sight unseen!

Chapter 30

THE LAND OF SOMEDAY

Well, I have three dates planned! I just decided that I should allow myself the luxury of at least meeting some of the men I have been dreaming of. I have a date, for lack of a better word, with Mr. BrownEyes for drinks and appetizers. I have a meeting scheduled for coffee with Mr. MarketingMan, and I have a meeting scheduled with Mr. Bonsai. I go deep into my heart to see if I have any feelings for any of them, but my curiosity and my nervousness kick in.

This may sound strange, but I am worried that I will lose them as pen pals if the meeting doesn't go well! Am I the only one who gets comfort from writing to strangers? During the "courting" stage, these men try so hard to give you their best. Some lie, but some are honest and want you to really get to know them. I love that and have really enjoyed the correspondence piece of all this.

In actuality a romantic relationship with so many men would be out of the question. It is a bit like interviewing people for a job. You can really enjoy meeting each candidate, but you only want to choose one. I think my heart has already chosen the General, so the ritual of meeting all these men is just like practicing dance.

I certainly don't want to be with or fall for multiple men, but there is a salient quality in each of these men that attracts me to them. Mr. Bonsai fills my heart with music every day, and he is really great with the subtle innuendos and quick quips that make me laugh, and oh how I need to laugh. Mr. BrownEyes is action oriented. He wrote, he called, he set the date. He knows that until we meet, there is no relationship. I like his decisiveness. Mr. MarketingMan is interesting. He enjoys a broad spectrum of activities now that he is retired, and he had the kind of career that was both creative and secure. I like his brain, and think it is funny that someone whose career was all about creating images and brands for others, gets his point across with one-liners. He, too, did not waste any time making a date.

The lesson here is to grab life by the collar and make it work for you. What are you really waiting for? If you are living in the past, filled with jilted love, messy divorce or death of a spouse, know that the past is gone. You can't go back; you can't reclaim any of the events. You have no power to change it in any way.

Today is all we have. We need to live it, love it, and good or bad, we need to know that we have power over today. We can create the best day by simply having direction and staying in action. Sure, we can dwell in the safety of anonymity and take some sense of security in all those pen pal relationships, but can we really? Don't you want to hear those voices, feel those hands, experience the intellectual exchange of words, sense the spirit of the person, and even taste their lips? (Come on, you know you do!) How can any of those things happen when you sit watching your life go by through a series of emails?

Can any of us afford to give up this day, the only day we are sure of? Yet so many live life like we have endless time granted to us. We put up roadblocks to prevent our own happiness. We live in the land of "what if" and "someday." Today is precious. It is all we have.

We punish ourselves by our fear and our indecision. We throw away the only thing that is real…these twenty-four hours. What are you going to do today that will make your life different from yesterday? Will you meet one of your many pen pals for coffee? Will you turn off your computer and do something creative? Will you clean up your mess and start anew? Will you give of yourself to someone who has less than you? Will you stop complaining about a piece of your life and change it?

Each and every one of us has the power and the right to live a fantastic life, and yet, so many give up their power. If you believe, as I do, that there is a Power greater than me who created all of this, then don't you think you are insulting that Power by not embracing your life? I heard a wonderful notion: God loves and supports us. He is by our side in everything we do. He has given us His seal of approval and the way you know that is by every beat of your heart!

Think about it. With every beat of our hearts we have the opportunity to live life to its fullest. We have the capacity and responsibility to love others and ourselves, and we have another precious moment to make a difference. Shut off your computer. Pick up the phone. Set a date. Grab the opportunity to meet someone in the flesh and learn to love again. Throw away all that old baggage. You no longer need to be that person ever again, nor do you have to wear a sign that says, "I messed up before," or "I was hurt in the past." Remember, we have no power over the past. Today, this glorious day, when you opened your eyes and your heart was still beating, today is the day to live your life and love your life. Don't throw that away!

Chapter 31

UNCOVERING THE LIES

I have been plagued by phone calls, emails and text messages from Mr. Dad. I decided that I really needed to end it all. I took the time to send him an email telling him that I wasn't comfortable in the relationship. I have too much work to do to be on a leash, and I need a relationship that is easy. I am independent and need to be. I am growing a business, and although I am happy for him, I do not need to know what kind of money he is making. He writes back that he doesn't understand. He is not demanding! He just wants to be close to me and he wants to always be honest. I try another approach, and another, until he says he understands. He then tells me it is his son's birthday, and he will take him out to celebrate. They are traveling in the Pacific, and it is very beautiful there. He promises to send me photos. I am a bit calmer, but I still want no part of this relationship. I have a bad feeling about him.

Later in the day, Mr. BrownEyes calls to say he is ill and our plans to meet for drinks have to be put on hold. I understand but am disappointed. I wonder if it is just an excuse. We will see.

I set a date to see Mr. Bonsai in the morning. I am excited. He has such a great way with words, and since I lost my favorite sparring partner, Mr. Lack of Technology, Mr. Bonsai has certainly taken his place. He seems to be excited, as well. He sends me some great music videos. I enjoy them and all the email exchanges, but I hope that we will stay pen pals no matter what happens tomorrow. I know it sounds weird, but if there is no physical chemistry between us, I hope we will remain friends.

I am deeply engrossed in a letter from the General. He tells me a story of a very expensive gift he has been given and he is unable to claim it because of where he is. He wants me to send money to get the gift released to me. He wants me to hold on to it until his return. I go cold. Could it be that this man with whom I have fallen in love is also going to try to scam me out of money? The wall goes up, and I have to tell him no. I try not to point fingers at him, but I simply say that I cannot take part in this (whether it is legal or not). Part of me is so angry to be in this position, and part of me is sad because I am imagining that this will end our relationship and I don't want it to end. I send the email, but I think that maybe he will write back. I feel like I have been run over by a bus.

My entire body hurts. I have such pain in my stomach and I am shaking with worry. How could he do this to me? He is the only one who actually seemed sincere. His love letters were so beautiful. He was so beautiful…or so I thought.

I am completely confused and have decided not to make any decisions. I will wait until the morning to see what happens. But I cannot wait until morning. I write a letter that points a finger at what a scam this is and how disappointed I am that he and I have exchanged nearly 100 emails and now he is pulling a scam for money. Why did he waste so much time? Shame on him for tricking me! I want no part of this.

Well, he writes back in an incredible rage. He is angry and feels disrespected

108

by my words. How dare I talk to him that way! He tells me to never email him again. Although I am crushed, I send an immediate reply.

I thought I had found love in you, but it has been man after man asking for money. How am I to decide who is real and who is not? I had hoped you were different. I guess I needed that. Your email threw me right back into indecision. I was so hurt that you would ask me to do something that I would feel is dangerous.

If there is anything true and real about all that has been between us, I hope you will honor that, and I hope you will continue to show me the real you. I certainly do not want to give up on a real relationship, but I think you understand that all this online stuff has such an element of the unreal that we both have to be guarded. We are both in a very reactionary place right now and using a computer does not make it any easier. I will respect that you are as hurt as I am, and I hope that when we each calm down, we can see through this misunderstanding. I want all that we have shared to be real, and I think you do too. I laid out my heart for you to take and you did. I can only tell you that if that meant anything to you, you would understand how scared I was.

I hope you will think about this and about me and all that has transpired. If it is in your heart to see why I was so scared by what you asked, and why I reacted the way I did, then I hope you will reach out again to try to resolve this and restore what seemed to be a very good thing for us both. If not, I think we will both lose, but I will respect your decision. I will never regret the time we took to get to know each other and all the hopes we had that we had found the right one with whom to grow a new life. I am very real and hope you will respect my feelings. We have hurt each other, not intentionally, but the hurt is real. If you feel any love at all for the woman you have grown to know, I hope you will think about all of this. If there is love between us, this will work out. I send you loving hugs for your safety.

Chapter 32

BEING YOU

I am so glad I sent that email because the email I got back in return was so beautiful and so loving. He melted my heart and restored my faith in him. He made it very clear that he still loved me and he would find other means of support. I breathed a guarded sigh of relief. I was shaken by his rage and calmed by his love. My head was spinning. I need to shake it all off. The interesting thing is that I have such deep feelings for him that I want to believe everything he says. I even rack my brain to think of how I might be able to help him!

Well, I have a bit of distraction in the form of a date with Mr. Marketing Man. We meet and talk for hours. It was such fun, but I don't think the sparks were flying. I think we will probably get together again but have no idea if we will ever be more than friends. I have learned to let things flow and not try to guess where things are going. I let things just be easy.

One of the happiest parts of all of this is that Mr. Lack of Technology is back. I so love his emails. He is so smart and really appeals to my intellectual side. He has of late been suggesting a romantic interlude. What? Wasn't he the one who slammed the door on me the last time we got to this place? This time he seems to be more serious. He is very respectful, and yet he describes what he hopes we will do.

This is all very interesting. Here is the man whose mind I adore, now telling me that a platonic relationship just isn't enough! This is too much to think about, so I initially retreat to my school-girl corner where I can hide from all of those female needs in the hope of protecting my reputation! He laughs at me and calls me a Born-Again-Virgin. Touché. I deserved that!

He is now telling me about menthol loofah scrubs and how he doesn't feel like a man unless he makes a woman feel like she is glad to be a real woman! Now who's aroused???? This is all well and good, but we still have not set a date to meet! Time will tell what comes next with this man. I can't really lose since I love his mind so much. He makes me laugh and he really makes me think. We fascinate each other and whether we keep things platonic or not, we are developing a great bond.

Friends with or without benefits is fine with me. I enjoy the complexity of this relationship. I don't think he would ever bore me. His mind is sharp, and his wit is quick...a perfect match. Will we take the relationship to another level? I have no idea and won't even venture to guess. If we do, we are both adults...actually senior citizens! His theory is that at our age, reputation is never questioned; we are simply fulfilling our needs.

The newest guy on the scene is The Frenchman! He is a riot! He writes to me in French. I love it, but boy do I have to struggle to figure out what he is saying. It has been sooo long since I have had to use that language skill. He is fun, brief in his comments, but I can almost see the twinkle in his eye! In my response to his question about what I was doing this weekend, I told him I needed to work at an event. His response, "What are you, the eye candy?" Cute flirt! Quick wit. Love it!

All these amazing men! Normally, I would be embarrassed about this and beating myself up for even considering going out with them, but I am just starting to realize how deprived of fun I have been. It's the kind of fun that a man's flirt, attention and touch can bring. Each of these men is so different, but each has a very special place in my heart. I will do everything in my power not to hurt any of them, but for now, I am going to enjoy the variety and the substance of each relationship.

I am learning what a truly complex woman I am. These men are showing me that it is okay to be complex. It is okay to be smart, funny, beautiful and sexual. It is more than okay; it is a God-given right.

In getting to know all these men, I have come to realize that they simply think differently than I do. For them, sex is simply sex. They have no need to attach any more to it than their need to satisfy their urges. They don't want any drama, nor do they need to be convinced to have it. They feel the urge and they do whatever is necessary to fulfill their needs. Some even have the attitude that sexual urges are given to us by God. They are life's free pleasures. They are a gift.

My thought process is so different. There is a strong mind component to it all. I need to hear and see sexual innuendos to start the process going. I need to feel a man's touch and experience the warmth of his kisses. My arousal comes over time and with visual and sensual stimulation. A man can simply think "I'm horny" and go after what he wants. When I am playing coy, flirting or touching a man, I am leading up to intimacy. A man can be there and back before I get to where I need to be.

Some men are truly sensitive and can pace themselves to match the pace of a woman. They enjoy pleasing the woman so much that their pleasure is tied to hers. Somehow, I think Mr. Lack of Technology might just be like that. He holds all the cards in this relationship, so I know that there is the possibility that I will never meet him, but that will be okay. Mr. Bonsai is a constant source of joy. He has music in his heart, and every night he sends me a serenade. I love it and have enjoyed getting to know him. We are becoming good friends...and I have even met him!

By the end of the day, things have heated up with the General. He is back to needing some money and I am back to resisting. I just don't want to start a relationship this way. I have no guarantee that anything I hear online is real. I do not want to risk my money for something so uncertain. I don't like the way I feel and I especially do not like the fact that I feel the relationship will come to a crashing halt if I tell him I cannot do what he asks. I simply have adopted a "we'll see" attitude. I will not place any scripts on it. I am simply going to let it play out. If he is truly in love with me, it will work out. I cannot worry about any of this.

Today an Italian Stallion shows up to play. He is really funny, but I think he may be too fast for me. This Born-Again-Virgin definitely is going at a different pace than he is. I want romance. He is an in-your-face kind of guy. Sex, sex, and more sex. Can't really tell if all that's true, but that's how he presents himself.

This is where I like the anonymity. I can be at home and imagine all he says without actually being pressured into doing anything. It is like reading a Harlequin romance, but the difference is that there is the possibility of it coming true!

Wonder if there will ever be a "Fabio" in my life! A sad thought comes over me. What if Mr. Niceguy is my "Fabio" and I've thrown him away? I miss his tenderness. I miss his loving embraces and those deep soulful kisses. I really miss the way he is so protective of me. He worries about me in all aspects of my life. He is clearly deep in my heart. On a certain level I love him, but he's not mine. I have lots of pen pals still.

The General, with all of our problems, is still with me, and we email or IM daily. I want him to be real, and yet there are days when I have my doubts.

Mr. Niceguy will always be in my heart and we will remain friends though we both want more. Mr. Lack of Technology is probably the best match for me in many ways, but he is so shy, never aloof, just shy. I love the way he can lead me into a fantasy world and then, after some contemplation, he apologizes. He, too, has my heart. I hope he will one day be ready to meet me because I think we could be friends, good, good friends.

The Italian Stallion is forever present at the moment, but he is a bit of work to calm down. His libido is through the roof. He makes me laugh, and, when he stops being hyper-sexual, he is sweet and tender. He and I are no match at all. On lots of levels we are simply opposites. No ying to my yang. He is what most would conclude the epitome of online dating, a guy with such high sex drive that he is probably married and can't ever get enough, so he cruises the online world to satisfy his needs. A sweet, single woman's nightmare.

Mr. MarketingMan wants to meet again, and we will have a great conversation like old friends. We talk as if we know everything about each other and are very comfortable. It is fun to have that kind of relationship. In his writing, he is also the king of exclamation points!!!!!!!!!!!!!

The Frenchman is so funny. He sends me one-liners that make me fall off my chair laughing. He and I will finally meet, or so he says. I think he will be fun and frisky in person. Maybe too "frisky." We'll see if he is yet another shy guy who thought he wanted a date, but in reality, can only handle a new pen pal.

Today there is a new guy in town, The Writer. He is so adorable and so smart. We exchanged many emails today. We talked all about the writing process and how to get published; we talked about education and shared theories about the most famous psychologists like Freud and Adler.

I have realized that I get extremely excited when the man is well-read and truly has a great mind. I guess that disqualifies me from being the perfect online date. Too nerdy. I am not online for the sex, and those who really need a woman like that fall away quickly. They are repulsed by me and usually move on.

I love emailing The Writer, but of course, he is way too young for me. I think I just have too much energy for my age! And there always has to be one with a dark side. The Chef! What a strange man. He called me every sort of name in the book. He told me I am judgmental, self-centered, and pompous and then he said how could I ever be his "business partner" and write a cookbook with him! With every email, he became more and more angry. I could not believe what he was doing, and I could not believe his answers. It came to a screeching halt, thank goodness!

This is where you are wondering why I responded at all to such insulting emails. Why don't I simply just drop it when I see the direction in which it is going? I am so fascinated in the study of human nature that I am drawn into keeping the conversation going, for just a little while, to see where it will go. The email exchange I had with the Chef was like we were on two different planes of thought. I won't lay any blame on him here; I simply feel that our personalities were so different that whenever I said something, he would read it differently than the intention with which it was written and answer in a way that I would take to be bizarre.

Chapter 33

WHAT ARE YOUR BOUNDARIES?

I woke up exhausted and pensive. I can't stop thinking about Mr. Lack of Technology and how much I care about him. I don't know why I feel so close to him, I haven't even seen his face. I guess what I have seen is his heart, and I love what I see. He sometimes goes into fantasy mode and then, being the true gentleman that he is, beats himself up for going there. He feels that if he dreams about being more than pen pals, he is being disrespectful to me and to himself. The interesting thing is that, even in his fantasy world, he is always respectful. He just doesn't see it.

He is holding on to a lot of hurt from a marriage gone bad. He is separated from his wife, but not from the prison associated with the marriage. I am so pensive this morning that I can't resist. I write him this letter:

> *You've given me so much to think about. I was hiding under a basket for many years during my marriage. On the outside everyone thought I was fine, but on the inside, I stopped dreaming that there could be a better life for me. Endurance was the theme of my existence. In the past two years, I have learned that I was*

blessed with many things and I had no right to turn my back on the person God made me to be. I stopped allowing myself to hide. I stepped into my own skin and started to live a more authentic life. I owe it to God to be the best I can be and I know that I deserve all of the gifts in life, like love and happiness.

You owe it to yourself to live without feeling the need to beat yourself up if you feel happy - even if that happiness is associated with something to which you have assigned a negative emotion like "cheating." Maybe the act of making a decision about your life and all you deserve will set you free. "Separation" is a form of indecision. You have put yourself in a kind of prison because you are not free in your mind to live and love fully. You see yourself shackled by the bonds of a bad marriage; yet you are not free to live. I do feel that indecision is a form of self-abuse.

I know I am saying some really hard things, but my heart goes out to you. You deserve to live fully. You deserve to dream and experience all the wonderful things in life. Soon you will have a grandchild and you will feel hope. You will dream of all the best in life for that precious baby. You need to get a baby picture of yourself and dream of all the best in life for the precious baby inside you. We have nothing but today. Live it fully. Create a life that you can love...you deserve it.

This Eagles' song is my favorite. It was my focus song 16 years ago when I had cancer. I would not go into treatment until I had heard it straight through. I still love the lyrics:

> I was standing all alone against the world outside
> You were searching for a place to hide
> Lost and lonely now you've given me the will to survive
> When we're hungry love will keep us alive
> Don't you worry sometimes you've just got to let it ride

118

The world is changing right before your eyes.

Now I've found you, there's no more emptiness inside

When we're hungry love will keep us alive

I would die for you, climb the highest mountain.

Baby, there's nothing I wouldn't do.

Lost and lonely now you've given me the will to survive.

When we're hungry love will keep us alive

I would die for you, climb the highest mountain.

Baby, there's nothing I wouldn't do.

Lost and lonely now you've given me the will to survive.

When we're hungry love will keep us alive

Lost and lonely now you've given me the will to survive.

When we're hungry love will keep us alive

When we're hungry love will keep us alive

When we're hungry love will keep us alive.

I care about you, my friend, and my wish is that you find peace in your heart about your marriage. Sometimes we carry around old stories that don't serve us well. We need to throw away the old stories and step into our own skin to live a rich, robust, and yet totally respectful life.

Some people look at me as frenetic because I do all I do. I think I owe it to God to discover my path and what I was meant to do. My prayer every day is: God use me up. Help me to discover and use all the talents you have given me and help me to be a reflection of all the good that you have instilled in me.

I have been writing for more than thirty days and have spent many an hour pondering the intricacies of relationships. What are we really all looking for? Perhaps it is unfair that I categorize the men who have dropped into my virtual life, but I have seen patterns that have repeated themselves over and over.

Some are strictly overt <u>sex mongers</u>. They cruise the site for anyone who will say yes to their advances. They are not looking for a relationship, just a way to satisfy their raging libidos.

Some are <u>sycophants and thieves</u>. They send photos that are not their own and try to lure a woman into sending them some money for a made-up emergency.

Some are so <u>introverted</u> that although they are on a "dating" site, they will never actually ask anyone out. They have so many negative scripts going on in their heads that they are powerless to move out of anonymity and into the socially adept face-to-face world. If they like a woman, they become her pen pal, and, if they are lucky, a friendship of sorts will ensue.

Some are <u>religious zealots</u> who tell you that God has sent you to them and you need to be together because it is God's plan. Some even go so far as to say they will read you the scriptures every night.

Some are <u>authentically looking</u> for that one woman who will make them feel whole. Often, they have had a good relationship with a woman before and want to have one again. Many have lost their wives and are very much in need of companionship. They believe that there is one woman out there who will bring them love and happiness. They take their time because the online world is scary. They view it as a double-edged sword, loving the sense of danger and intrigue, while hoping, all the time, not to get hurt.

How do I view relationships? In the most simplistic form, a relationship is a heart connection that often starts with a meeting of the minds. The intellectual match is powerful for me. Without it, I don't know if I would even open myself up enough to allow a heart connection to form.

I want to instantly smile and feel my heart soften and skip a beat every time the person comes to mind and every time I see them, and I want them to feel the same about me. I love that look of openness and warmth I see when I enter the room and someone there loves me. I love having someone with whom I can talk for hours or sit silently with and feel the strength of their love. I love that feeling of mutual trust that, even on the worst of days, everything will be okay because of our bond, our unity. I love the full spectrum of emotions from gentle tenderness to raging passion and all the shades of feelings in between. I love the knowing looks that silently say it all from "not now" to "take me I'm yours"! A bond that is so powerful that it can only exist between people who are connected in mind, body, and soul. Relationships are about having someone with whom to share your passions and beliefs. I also believe that the purpose of a relationship is not to have another who might complete you, but to have another with whom you might share your completeness.

Chapter 34

APPEALING CHARACTERISTICS

I get the sweetest note from Mr. BrownEyes. He writes to tell me he doesn't want to keep me waiting. He thinks he has found "HER." He really hopes we can be friends. I answer that I am thrilled and of course we can be friends. Isn't it refreshing to see how a mature gentleman handles things? Don't you wish all "break-ups" could end in this way? His note gives me hope that there are more nice guys out there like him. Every day there are countless new men sending me emails and flirts. Far too many to include here since they will be in and out of my life with the click of a mouse.

If I were to sum up my experience and where I stand after a month, it would be that I have a strong pull on my heartstrings by Mr. Niceguy, Mr. Lack of Technology and The General. They each have a piece of my heart, and I am torn over each of them. Everyday Mr. Niceguy calls me to tell me how much he misses me and wants me. I have been resisting, but I am not sure if that is wise. There are so many things about this man that make him great for me. I see how much he loves me by the way his eyes melt when he sees me. He must be touching me whenever we are together. He melts my heart. He gives me good advice, and I know I could trust him with anything.

Mr. Lack of Technology is the most profound of all the men. His mind really turns me on. I love that we can have philosophical debates, and neither of us has to win! I love his heart and long to meet him. I long to be wrapped in his arms. We have a definite connection. We email each other at least once or twice a day. Oh, if I could only get him to meet me.

Mr. Bonsai is my true delight. We email five or more times a day. He sends me serenades, and he, too, gives me good advice. I am so comfortable with him. We share stories of our online adventures. We comfort each other when a date stands us up or does something to hurt us. In my heart, I think this will never be more than a good friendship, but I have been known to be wrong in the past. I really like him, and that's good enough for me.

Mr. MarketingMan is also a friend. He has set another date for us to meet. I am comfortable with him and feel open to seeing where this will go. He is simply a nice guy.

Chapter 35

WHAT'S REAL?

The General has spent the better part of the month gradually growing an online love for me. He writes me such profoundly beautiful love letters. He is bright, and I get the sense that he would always be true to me and to himself. His needing money is certainly of concern to me, but what if he is being totally honest and I am rejecting him? He, too, turns me on by his brilliance. He is also a mystery. I just got to a place where I was falling in love with him, and I was about ready to part with the money he claims to need, if he would provide me with some protection that I would neither get in trouble with the deal, nor would I lose the money. Love can do very strange things to your head. The thing I hated the most was the very thing he asked for. Should I hold on to my power and not give him any money or should I let it all go?

Well, today was like most, a new collection of possible suitors and probable characters in this book. I was online for a while when I got a flirt from someone whose profile matched the General's and whose face matched his as well! There he was on his motorcycle, with a new ID and new name, flirting with me! What! Was he crazy? Why would he do that? What was that all about? Could he really be that careless if he were a cheater? I was shocked and didn't know what to do. Where had all the love gone? How could he have written more than 100 emails and apparently fall in love with me? What was going on? I answered his email by saying that this was a surprise and followed up by saying that I hoped he would have fun with all his profiles. I couldn't resist emailing him this letter:

Well, you know I can't resist writing to you! I am curious, really curious about what happened? How could someone as intelligent as you send me a flirt using another online profile name? You email me at Heartfelt and Heartfelt is my IM ID as it is also my online ID. How could you have forgotten who I was and send me that flirt? Was it simply your way of ending things, knowing that I would not be interested in someone who misrepresented himself? It is hard for me to believe that you would have unknowingly made such a glaring mistake.

Well, Michael or Thomas or whatever your real name is, it's been fun, and I wish you all the best. I am sure you will find the woman with whom you were meant to spend the rest of your life. She's out there. You did a great job writing your profile…someone will melt over it. (Oh, wait, should I have Googled it to see where it came from?) The interesting thing is I am not the least bit angry. I might have been if I had found out after I met you, or after I gave you $2,000. That might have brought me pause. The online world is so full of trickery and deceit that this seems to be only another familiar scenario.

If I can figure out where to send it, I will surely send you a copy of the book so that you can read all about our "love affair" from my perspective. I think you might enjoy it…it will make you laugh now that you have revealed yourself. But be careful; there are some women who take things very hard. I get the sense that, no matter who you really are, you would not actually want to be responsible for another person's demise...a little money exchange, maybe, but not their total demise. Wishing you all the best.

I figured that I should take the high road in all this. No need to bother with all the drama associated with being lied to and finding out about it. I was glad that he gave me a reality kick in the butt. I was contemplating giving him the money and would have been so angry with myself if I had. He did me a favor. It is always better to know what you are getting into before you make a serious commitment.

This dose of reality reminded me that I was getting off course. I know better than to believe everything I read in an email. Heck, I'm a writer and sometimes it just feels good to embellish the truth.

I got whisked away by the power of my mind. I heard the words in an email through my voice, and not through the voice of the reader. I let my vivid imagination and my desire to be loved work in combination to help me believe that what I wanted was in fact exactly what this man had to offer. I wasn't angry with myself because I hadn't given him anything at all - not me, not my body, and not my money. I had simply invested some hours into seeing if we were a match. I gained more perspective into what I wanted in a man and what I needed to hear from him.

There was a gift in all of this. I learned that I have the capacity to love and not be taken advantage of. I no longer need to give to a man who can't reciprocate. I did that for far too long. I can be loved, and I can love, without losing myself.

There was nothing real about the situation with the General. I just needed what he stood for. In the end, he was the antithesis of that. I see no strength, no responsibility, no honesty, and no honor in anything he did. All the traits I thought he had were made up. He played the game right to the bitter end. He came online again as Thomas, pretending not to know me or anything about my situation. He was a bold-faced liar, professing not to know who Michael Lindsay was, even though they had exactly the same profile.

Maybe tomorrow I will be angry or sad or something else, but for today I am simply relieved that it did not go further. I can still walk away with my head held high, and I can stand a bit taller, knowing that I did not do anything stupid that I would have to regret. Well, maybe one really stupid thing; I sent him a very cryptic IM message:

Nice one! I didn't see that coming. Very creative! The writer in me loved the twisted plot. We really should write a book together. You could take them on a very twisted journey and then simply walk away. It would be a bestseller.

Mr. Niceguy, Mr. Bonsai, Mr. Marketing Man and Mr. Lack of Technology don't seem to be cut from the same cloth as The General, and for that I am thankful. I probably should report him, but who would I report? I am sure that both names are made up. At best, I can report and block them on the dating site. I am sure he is off trying to woo another woman to get her money or simply to have the bragging rights to say he won her heart.

I don't really know what makes a man like that tick, and, truth be told, I don't really want to know. What a waste of a creative mind. Instead of using all that brain power for good, he uses it for evil. He claims to be a part of one of the most honorable organizations in the United States, and he is nothing but a lying cheat.

He was good, and he worked hard to woo me back. He told me all the truths and all of the lies and begged me to forgive him. He vowed that he had lied earlier and would never lie to me again. He professed allegiance to me and begged me to be open-minded. He would prove to me that he was real, and he was honest…and I believed him. I don't know why. Maybe I just needed to believe that he would never do this to me again. He and I had exchanged so many emails that I felt something for him. I wanted him to be real. My heart was breaking! Had I seriously fallen so completely for this man that I would believe anything? Could I ever trust him again?

This morning, another guy is trying to steal my heart. He is convinced we will live happily ever after! Did I miss something? I was under the assumption that you needed to meet someone before you would know that you could live happily ever after with them. Who knew it was so easy! Just get an email address and voila! You are linked for life. Do you hear that???? Are those wedding bells and chirping birds?

I was always cynical before, but now I am way over the top! I kind of like reality; besides, if we were to stereotype, isn't it a girly thing to want Prince Charming to sweep you off your feet and carry you into the sunset? What's with all of these men? I kind of like my Swamp Yankee guy who teaches me how to fix my tractor through a series of emails and ends the conversation with, "Let me be your dipstick, Baby! " At least if we sailed off into the sunset, it would be on a boat!

Chapter 36

WHOSE BEHAVIOR NEEDS TO CHANGE?

I woke up this morning thinking about my life and how many things had changed in one short month. I feel that for so many years I had the "pause" button on. I had not been happy in my marriage, and so I just hit "pause" and silenced that part of my life. I did nothing to create an opportunity for new love and romance because I was just stuck. I saw no way out. I thought that because of some Catholic guilt, I needed to stay married and faithful to a man who gave me nothing.

I blamed myself for the marriage being so bad, but I had truly gotten to the point where I had no interest in making it better. I didn't want to try because I saw no hope. I thought that it would be impossible for my husband to change, and I had turned away from the belief that if you change your behavior in a relationship of any kind, the relationship will automatically change.

Most of us spend so much time trying to change the behavior of others when, in reality, the only behavior we can change is our own. We have total control of our thoughts, our beliefs, and our actions. If we don't like the way our relationships are going, we need to change our own approach to them.

Give what you want to receive and know that each of us has an internal clock. It guides the timing of our actions and is the thing that frustrates us most when we want something now to satisfy that need for instant gratification. The best way to be on the same page with another person is simply through good communication. Just ask them what they like and what they need and tell them what you need. It is so simple, yet it seems that so many people fail to communicate well.

Chapter 37

MONEY

I didn't want to talk about money, but the longer I talk with people about online dating, the more the topic of money comes up. Oh, sure, there are the fees (some of which are ridiculously high) that you need to pay to join the sites, but that's not what I am talking about. I have heard story after story about women who have given the fictional "man of their dreams" excessive amounts of money to bring them to this country, or to put a deposit down on a house for the two of them. We are talking amounts in excess of one million dollars!

For those of us who, as a rule, don't lend money to others, this news is staggering. It is especially sad when you know that the woman has never even met this man. I know that some of the men are great crafters of stories, truly heartbreaking stories that demonstrate how they are suddenly in a desperate situation and need money instantly. Remember the story about the man who wanted me to send money for oxygen to save his son? I knew it was fabricated, and so I did not fall for it.

I have spent a lot of time trying to come up with the reason anyone would send money to a stranger, even if he tells her, he loves her. Are there really so many gullible women out there who believe everything they are told? My theory is that all these scenarios that demonstrate how a woman would give away her money are examples of a really poor sense of self-worth. Ladies, you deserve to be treated better than that!

I understand you are on a dating site because you are lonely and want to find someone who will love you, but do you really want to be involved with a man who abuses you and takes from you, just to feel you are loved? You do realize that there is no end to the things these men will take from you, and all they have to do is tell you they love you! Love yourself first!

A true partner would never treat you in a way that would hurt you. A partner wants you to be safe and happy. Most men have a very protective nature, and the honest ones will love you as you are. They will not love you for your money or your belongings. They will not love you just for the physical pleasures you give them. They will encourage you to move your life forward. Hopefully, their goal will be to create memories together with you, not to be your worst nightmare.

Take your time, I know you want to give this man everything you can to bond with him and show him you love him, but if he authentically loves you, he will never just ask you for money. Trust me, the minute you wire him money, you will never hear from him again!

Chapter 38

LEARNINGS, DISAPPOINTMENTS AND AHA MOMENTS

"It's your road, and yours alone, others may walk it with you, but no one can walk it for you."

Rumi

My original intent for writing this book was to help other women. I never knew what my journey would be when I started. I thought a month of documenting everything would be enough, but as you might realize, it certainly wasn't. I started the book several years ago, and since that time I have had some major ups and downs. I fell in and out of love with a man and had three or four men try to scam money from me. I have really found some wonderful new friends who I think will be friends for life. I have learned a lot about protecting myself, but it is also my way to poke fun at myself and all the "Italian Stallions" and "Hey, Baby" guys who think they are cool in the eyes of a woman.

Because of all the motivational training I've had, there are lots of places in the book where I help people look at the "why" that drives them to

133

the online world and whether or not they are being true to themselves. People need connections, but for most of us, our path to getting the most authentic, supportive connections, is often fraught with pain.

For some reason, we seem to want to take the fast track to the everlasting. I have always believed that until we are whole and stable as individuals, we shouldn't venture into couplehood. There are so many different types of connections that are supportive and satisfying without being the "everlasting love" connection. Why limit the search to that?

I must include the story about the funniest date I went on. I will call this man Dale. He was eighty years old, spry, and very active, going to senior citizen events and doing volunteer work all the time. Dale and I had such fun talking on the phone for weeks before we decided to meet. We set a date to meet on the deck of my favorite restaurant on Long Island Sound. Dale told me that I would recognize him because he would be carrying an orange! I laughed and told him that I had gotten flowers before, but never an orange! "I could make it a watermelon!" said Dale. On the night of our date, the weather was beautiful - a great evening to eat by the water. As I approached the deck, I spotted a man with an orange! When I sat down, Dale handed me the orange, a gorgeous bouquet of flowers, and half a watermelon!!! Although we weren't each other's types, I will never forget the fun I had that night from this creative, romantic, octogenarian!

The thing I've learned is not to put any pressure on myself. Do I think there is a man out there for me? It is absolutely the thing I believe in the most.

I want this book to be helpful for you. Here are some things I have learned about SCAMMERS:

1. First and foremost, SCAMMERS have patterns. They all have wives who died 6 years ago, either from cancer or in a car accident on the way home from church. Their wives were either nurses or teachers.

2. They usually have an only child who may live in Europe. Are you sobbing yet???

3. They write the most beautiful and romantic notes to you daily. They always know exactly the right words to say. They know when you are down (it's your Achilles heel) and will come to your aid to cheer you up with their love.

4. They send you songs to listen to that are profoundly beautiful.

5. Many of them profess to be construction workers or civil engineers.

6. They own their own companies and are doing their final project before retiring.

7. The jobs are always in Europe, Africa or Dubai. When they get there, everything has gone awry. They can't transfer money from their bank and need to borrow $29,000 from you! Do you get the picture? DO NOT, please, do not ever send one cent to them, especially if you have never met them.

8. Another way to spot scammers is to look at their writing. Their language skills aren't good. They write very poorly. They never put spaces after commas or periods like we do in the US. It's a great way to spot an imposter.

9. They make the excuse that they were raised in Europe and have an accent. The guys in huts in Africa claim to have an Italian accent. For some reason, they think an African accent sounds Italian.

10. They are also very quick to write you an elaborate email as soon as you say "Hi" to them.

11. They tell you how lucky they are to have found someone as beautiful as you are. Don't fall for it! Go look in the mirror and tell yourself how beautiful you are because you are! You deserve better than this.

I want this to be in bold letters: **YOU ARE ENOUGH**. *You deserve the best! I don't want anyone who reads this book to be scammed.*

Another thing you can do is study their pictures. If you aren't sure whether or not they are real pictures, you can take the image and do a Google image search to see if the photo belongs to someone famous. I had someone write to me for a long time who was using the photo of a famous playboy. When I finally caught him, I told him that not only did he owe me an apology, but he owed the playboy an apology as well.

Always, and I repeat, always, do a background search of anyone you meet online before meeting them in person. Sites like Spokeo will, for a fee, do a complete search for you. It will tell you if he has a criminal record, if he is still married, his driver's license number, etc. I don't care if it costs. It is worth the money! You may be shocked, but it may save your life!

Also, if they want to text you, copy the phone number, and put it into reverse phone lookup under Whitepages. Be sure to check everything. He may tell you he is in Florida when his number is from Montana and is listed to a name other than the one he has given you. Also, when you call him, dial *67, wait for the beeps and then dial his number. Your number will not come up on his caller ID.

I don't want to sound cynical because I'm not. Protect yourself. I have met some great guys. I have had coffee with a man for the past year. We have an intellectual relationship that I love. It is not a romantic relationship, but I love the time with him in which I don't have to dumb myself down when having a conversation. We talk about all sorts of things. We are both educators and have a lot in common. What started as an online date turned into a wonderful friendship.

There are all sorts of relationships. They don't all have to be about true love. You can have a Friend with Benefits relationship…and while we are on that topic, be sure before you are intimate with anyone to look at their STD report. I am not kidding! Insist you see that report. As a matter of fact, get yourself tested, as well. It's the fair thing to do.

Those of us born before 1960 never had to worry about HIV and STDs, but they are out there, and I don't want you to get hurt. A simple test can put your mind at ease.

I thank you for being smart enough to take good care. Go out there and have some fun, but the best way to meet a man is to go out and do the things you love to do. If you love to go on cruises, go on a singles cruise and meet a man. Go volunteer your time for Habitat for Humanity and swing a hammer next to a great guy who cares about the world like you do. Go to a self-development workshop. The men you meet there will be great men who are caring and sensitive, and who want to be better people.

Don't think the online world is the only place to meet a great guy. It is not. Dating sites are fun and frustrating, but when you are truly ready and when you least expect it, that wonderfully delicious relationship will come into your life, so put on your big girl panties and go out there to have some fun. I wish you Godspeed. I wish you a happy heart. I wish you love forever.

I am going to give you one last story. It is the biggest disappointment for me because this man was right for me on so many levels…except one. The story is called the Great Imposter. I will let you read it for yourself.

Chapter 39

THE GREAT IMPOSTER

Whatever would possess a highly intelligent, very successful man to go onto a dating site for overweight women and pretend to be someone he's not? He certainly isn't looking for money, and he isn't being forced into a relationship, so why would he lie about his name and who he is? Could he still be married? Is he a thief? Is he sadistic, wanting nothing more than to break an innocent woman's heart? Is he, God forbid, a serial killer waiting for the right moment to make his move?

You know the adage: If it seems too good to be true, then it is. Well, I went on a dating site for big, beautiful women and had a man contact me. He was very insistent that he wasn't a scammer and quickly offered his phone number and email address. He told me that he was really into plus-sized women; he loved my online profile and had to get to know me. "Just take a chance," he said. "I'm not a scammer. Here is my phone number and email address."

I usually just delete requests like that because they seem so insincere, but to my surprise, I answered him, and I called him. He was charming from the very beginning, not too hot and heavy with sexual implications, but appearing to sincerely want to get to know me. We talked that night for a very long time. We talked the next night and the next and the next. This went on for a while, building what seemed like an authentic relationship.

I hate men who are the "Hey, Baby" type. They want one thing and one thing only, and they don't even want to take the time to know your name, so they call every woman, "baby." He wasn't like that…and so I began to believe that he was real!

We spent many hours on the phone. He freely told me all about his family, his failed marriages, his love of his grandchildren and lots of other things that made him who he is today. He told me many stories about his younger days, and all he had been through and conquered. The longer we talked, the easier the relationship became. He started to call me "Sweetheart" and made comments on how intelligent and caring I am. He said that without a cerebral connection, there would never be a physical connection.

The longer we talked, the more my defensive wall came down. He seemed like just the person I would love to start a long-term relationship with. He had all the qualities I was looking for in a man. He was intelligent and had the same type of humor I have. He was romantic and loving. He was a business owner like me. He was well-educated and cultured. The more we talked, the more we both seemed to want to meet each other. The connection was there between us. He would call and serenade me with his made-up lyrics such as, "I just called to say I like you."

I was really softening. I was anxious to meet this man. I loved his voice and his personality and wanted to see if there was any physical chemistry between us. Over time our phone conversations became more suggestive. We discussed all sorts of things from our sexual preferences to pre-nuptial agreements! I felt I knew so much about him except how it would feel to be with him physically. We talked daily and for hours at a time. He started to talk about how much we needed to take things to the next level and meet so that we could determine if we wanted to go on.

The thing that is so unique about the online dating world is that, in real life, you would never start a relationship "interviewing" a potential partner to see what their political, religious, and sexual policies are. Being of an advanced age, there is the added element of the clock ticking and our not wanting to "waste" time. We want to get together right away so we can see if the person is a potential partner. We are far more decisive in our old age because of time constraints, and, whether real or implied, we just don't want to make stupid choices. Life is too precious and too short for us to waste it jumping from person to person.

We set a date to meet for an early dinner. He drove one and a half hours to meet me. He was parked in the parking lot of the restaurant when I arrived. We both got out of our cars, and because, as it turned out, the restaurant was closed, we chose another. But before we got back into our own cars, we kissed, and then we kissed again...long and soulful. There was an instant attraction, and the kiss that happened even before the hello was proof.

At the sushi restaurant he smiled and put his hands out over and over to take my hands in his. He caressed them each time, showing how he felt, even though no words were exchanged. He was charming, smiling at me and calling me "delicious." We laughed a lot, held hands a lot, and talked as if we had known each other forever. We really enjoyed the meal and our time together, and neither of us wanted the evening to end. I asked if he would like to come over for coffee since I lived less than two miles from the restaurant.

We got to my house, and he walked around looking at everything. He commented that he loved that it was a "real home." We enjoyed coffee, and then we began to make out. His kisses were intense and beautifully tender. I snuggled into his chest, wanting to do no more than feel his arms around me and listen to the beat of his heart. I was so comfortable with him. His hands began to roam all over my body. We both knew that no matter how much we wanted a sexual union, we would not go that far. It was too soon,

141

and we had agreed that we would each get tested for STDs before we were intimate with each other. After many, many kisses, we parted.

He continued to call me and text me every day, but shortly after our meeting, he announced that he had been invited to join his best friend on a two-week adventure to the southern Caribbean. His friend was getting divorced and had already paid for a cruise that his soon to be ex-wife would not be going on. My reaction was that, of course, it was fine with me, but this "sudden" cruise offer seemed to create doubts in my mind over the truthfulness of this venture. I really felt that he would just stop contacting me, but every time I was convinced that I would never hear from him again, he texted and called.

I was so confused! Was he real and sincere, or was he just a phony? I kept thinking that his words were too good to be true, but I didn't need to be stupid. Something caused me to doubt him. I was smart enough to do a background check on him to see what I could find out. I was well-aware of the potential dangers that can arise when getting too involved with an online stranger. In my heart I hoped that nothing negative would come up because, in that very same heart, I liked him and wanted to get to know the man he appeared to be.

I started an extensive search and came up with no one with that name. I checked social media sites, Google-searched his name, and still nothing. I felt so confused and upset, but there were many more avenues I could go down, even if he seemed invisible. No one is invisible these days! I had a lot of information that he had freely given me, so I began searching his middle name and anything else I could find. Well, I hit the jackpot. I found a man who matched many elements of his profile, but his name was completely different from the one I had been given.

I felt as if I had gotten a sucker punch in the stomach. Why did he feel the need to completely lie about his name, yet tell me about his son, his birthday, his ex-wives' names, the kind of business he is in? He even told me the area in which he lived. What was his game? Was he trying to phish? Was he planning on doing me harm? My research gave me much information. He had no criminal record, I could see the building he lived in, knew when he moved in and its exact location. I knew how much he sold his last house for, and I even knew his driver's license number! I found the address of his last wife, and his son. He was clearly intelligent, so what did he plan to do? Was he dangerous? Did he get in over his head and not know how to extract himself?

I had so many questions. My feelings were tossed around. I was angry and hurt by his lies, yet at the same time, I was full of excitement and on a mission to uncover all I could to solve this mystery! On the home front, he was his kind, sweet, loving self on the phone and when texting. Even before he left for his cruise, I knew all this information about him. I spent hours and hours pondering different scenarios, wondering what the truth was. I had the strong urge to confront him face-to-face but had such angst over doing that because I was worried that he might be dangerous. I thought so much about it that I told myself I should not worry for the two weeks he was supposedly on the cruise, and just see if he showed up again after the cruise.

Don't men understand that Smart Chicks do their research??? I have experienced so many men who lie through their teeth, I just don't get it! Are all the lies a way to get free sex from an unsuspecting woman? Is it an innate trait, where lying is so natural to them that they don't think twice about it? What happens when they lie and then find a woman they really want? How do they back out of the lie and expect the woman to carry on as if it is nothing? How can you ever believe a man like this? Perhaps he really didn't want me at all; he just loved the chase. Who knows!

I would be lying if I said I wasn't sad and a bit heartbroken. I really, really liked this man and felt that he and I could potentially be a solid match, but what was I supposed to do with the information I had? If he ever calls again, should I simply ignore him? Should I allow myself to see him again and find a way to confront him in the lie? What if he just didn't know when to tell me? What if he really wants to be with me, but what would I do to let him know I know who he really is? Again, I am worried about how safe he is.

I have always had the personality that pushes through challenges by facing them head on. It just seems so natural for me to meet him again and see if he would come forward with the information about who he is. Shall I trick him into admitting it? That's really not my style - ever! I am upfront and honest to a fault. I am very happy to have a few weeks to think about all of this. Before he "left on his cruise," he was making excuses that he would try to email me if the Internet signal was good. I told him not to worry at all and just have a great vacation. I meant that because I truly wanted some time to think, and whether he was going on a cruise with his pal or not, he planned to be out of my life for several weeks. I was hoping to use that time to figure out what I wanted to do next. It was a difficult and scary decision.

I thought about it every day and I plotted out several scenarios in which I could get him to tell me the truth. I would certainly feel better if he told me directly, rather than my trying to convince him to tell me. If he did tell me, what on earth would I do with that information? How could I tell him it didn't matter that he completely lied to me or that he was forgiven, and I would trust him going forward? There is simply no good solution to this problem that he created by lying. I understand wanting to protect your identity to the mass public, but once he met me, why didn't he just say, "I have a confession to make. I put a fake profile out online, but I like you and need you to know the truth."

Too much has already transpired between us for it to be easy for him to tell me and for me to forgive his dishonesty. If there is one thing I hate, it is being on an emotional Ferris wheel. I am pretty much a straight shooter (forgive my gun reference!). I say what I mean and mean what I say. I also like knowing where I stand with everyone. I love board games, card games and the like, but I really hate some of the gender games people play. They make me angry, and they sometimes back a person into a corner from which there is no escape. I feel that's pretty much where things are in this situation. No easy way out of a lie that has been going on for weeks.

Anyone who lies to that extent will probably not want to explain. He may just put his tail between his legs and go away. He may also follow the pattern of most men and vanish into silence, too immature to simply say we are not a match, or I need to move on. As of this writing, he has been gone for 8 days, and I think about him daily. I miss his voice, his sense of humor and his charm. I miss how happy he made me when we talked and how funny he was when we texted. As I write this, I am aware of how quickly I was drawn to him and how much I instantly liked him. I am also painfully aware of how difficult this situation is.

I have gone on many dates and have easily discounted many possible relationships because of a lack of chemistry. The reason this is so painful is that I feel there was chemistry on many levels. Perhaps I am simply a fool, or he is simply a brilliant imposter. He will return from his "cruise" next week, and I may never hear from him, but either way, the rest of the story will unfold soon, and I will either be ecstatic or saddened by the outcome. I have weathered many challenges and many health issues as an adult and have developed a personal mantra, "This is not the thing that will take me out!" I know that I will be fine no matter what happens.

With regard to relationships that go awry, I love the quote, "Don't cry because it ended; smile because it happened." I will look for the lessons this man brought to me, and I will move forward armed with a greater understanding of who I am and how strong I have become with or without him by my side.

To add to my confusion, he texted me once saying he was in Saint Thomas and thinking of me, and on the day that he was supposed to be back home, he texted me to say "hi" and tell me we would talk soon, and he would tell me all about the trip. Here we go! The rest of the story will unfold soon. I am bracing myself to be disappointed – more disappointed than I have been in years.

The most interesting thing that happened that was beyond belief was that I took my photo down from the dating site, and he no longer recognized me. Suddenly, he started to flirt with me and ask me to call him or give him my email so he could send me some pictures!! Of course, he had another email address and yet another name! He is a pathological liar. I have never experienced anyone who was so crooked, except for those guys who are in huts in Africa and claiming to be Italians! They seem to think that their accents sound like Italian accents.

Those scammers are the most romantic of all the liars. You would swoon over all the sweet words, songs, poems, and romantic quotes they will send to woo a woman in the hope she will give him money. I can't decide who is worse, the poor guy looking to get out of a hut and find a new life in America, or the guy who has it all and simply delights in head games where lying to women to woo them and break their hearts is his delight.

The Great Imposter even professes to be extremely religious! I wonder what God will have to say about that when my friend tries to get through the pearly gates. I wonder if he will use his despicable string of lies to convince God that he is really a good guy. Karma is a bitch! I wonder if, when September comes around, he will try to contact me before the Bible closes so that his sins will be forgiven. I wonder what the Talmudic teachings would say about him???

The funniest thing is that when we first met, I told him that no matter what happened between us (long before I knew of his lies) either I was brought in to teach him a lesson or he was there to teach me one. Perhaps we have each learned a lesson that will change how we move forward in life and love.

He suddenly must have realized that he had gotten caught in his lies because he started texting me to ask me what my profile ID was. He couldn't find it! I had taken it down when he started flirting with me under yet another name! The reality of his complex dishonesty was too much for me to take. I will never understand why he felt the need to lower himself to such despicable standards. He is so well-accomplished, so poised, and polished, so smart, and yet he can be categorized among the most revolting of men.

What could possibly have happened in his life that would drive him to be such a con artist? Why would he need to reduce all that is good about him and all that he has worked for into nothing but sycophancy? How can he have such little self-esteem as to reduce himself to lying about everything? How does he sleep at night? How many relationships does he carry that into? Does he lie to his son, his family, his business relationships…himself?

I love to write. For me, it is cathartic to express my thoughts and feelings on paper, and so this story had to be put into one of my books to serve as a lesson for the readers who may have never experienced a pathological liar. They should be warned. I will also send a copy of it to The Great Imposter. I know who he is. I have his address! I hope it will serve as a mirror for him to see how much he is damaging himself and how simply telling the truth will change his whole life. I see the good in him and if he could honor that in himself, he could find true happiness.

I have learned so many lessons, and yet I feel it is important that I not start to believe all men are just liars. I know there are some great guys out there… wish he had been one too.

Every time I feel I've told you enough, my friends, something new happens! Perhaps all the things that are happening to me are present in my life so that I can share them with you, and if we are very lucky there will be an aha moment in them from which we can each learn a lesson.

Well, just to spice things up, I sent a message to a new man on a dating site. He answered immediately and said he was getting ready to come to my town and would like to meet me. We communicated back and forth for a while and made plans to meet. I told him I would like to talk on the phone before we met. Well, our conversation was easy and exciting. He said he was coming to a theater near me to see a concert by Suitcase Junket. I had never heard of him and decided to look him up. I liked the music, so I agreed to meet to see the concert. He told me he would be flying his four-passenger plane down to my city and he would meet me at the café!

Does the universe know how much I love new and different stories to tell? Imagine my delight when I tell people that my date flew down to meet me. We had a great evening. There were a few incidents that made me believe that my latest date was affectionate. He would touch my arm when we talked and a few times he put his hands on my shoulders to ask if I could see the musician. When we left, things became stilted and uncomfortable. He seemed very standoffish. He attempted to hug me, but it didn't go well. He never offered to walk me to my car or anything. Later that night, I sent him a brief thank you text and he replied that he hoped the next time we could go somewhere very quiet to get to know each other better. I had no idea what to make of all that. I decided not to worry.

As I was leaving my date and the concert, I got a text from the Great Imposter! He had received the story I had sent him, and he wanted to talk! We made plans to talk the next day. When he called me, he apologized and said he couldn't bear my thinking that he was the monster I had portrayed in my story. He told me he had been stalked by a woman whom he had met online and so he stopped using his real name. He said that all his failed relationships had made him fear commitment and that although he was extremely attracted to me, he could never have a committed relationship with me or anyone else. Whether or not that was true, I must give him credit for manning up and admitting he was wrong to lie to me. It gave me confidence that there are still mature men out there who will apologize when wrong.

Chapter 40

SOULMATE OR SOUL FRIEND?

S o now you are probably going to ask me if I've found love. I have clearly learned many lessons about myself and about the online dating world. I know that I love the male perspective and that having lived with one man for 43 years, I didn't actually know there were men who could be exactly what I needed in life. I have loved several men. Each satisfied me on a very different level.

I have learned how to recognize that although their approaches are very different, you can always tell when a man authentically loves you. He goes into protective mode and wants to take care of you. He loves you for who you are and isn't the least bit uncomfortable showing you. Although each man's display of romance is very different, the common thread is that when he looks at you, he will make you melt. You will see that love in his eyes. He will delight in spending time with you and be as happy to talk you to sleep as he is eager to talk to you the next morning.

A man who really cares about you will never put you down. He will respect and honor the person you are. He will encourage you to grow and flourish without losing sight of the bond between you. You should look for the person who compliments the traits you have. A good relationship should always feel easy.

We often hear people say they are looking for their soulmate. They want to find someone who they trust completely, someone they can laugh or cry with, someone who will always have their back. It's everyone's dream to find that perfect person you want to spend your life with.

What they may not realize is that there may be no romance with that person even if you both make a concentrated effort to establish the relationship. The lack of romantic connection may be that the person is your Soul Friend, not your soulmate. It can be a very powerful relationship, but you will never truly be soulmates.

You would be very fortunate to find a Soul Friend in life, but don't make the mistake that there is something wrong. Your true Soul Friend will never turn into your soulmate. Why am I telling you this? When you think you have found your soulmate, you may have only found a Soul Friend, and you should never feel that you are a failure if you have no romantic relationship. This friend for life may be wonderful, but they will never be the soulmate you desire.

Many a woman has married her Soul Friend thinking that the romance would eventually appear, but it never did. The dilemma comes when she has to make a choice whether to stay with the marriage even though there is no romance or give up the best friendship she could ever hope for. I have been very blessed to have found a Soul Friend. I love him deeply. We talk often and openly about everything. We make each other laugh. We are committed to each other's happiness and have each other's backs. We will never be romantic partners. That chemistry doesn't exist between us, yet the relationship is strong and rewarding. I am blessed to have this man in my life.

What's next for me? My soulmate is on his way to me. I know it with every fiber of my being. I have enjoyed this time to take a look at myself and to get clear about who I am and what I need in a partner. You let the Universe know that you deserve the best when you take the time to be the best you can be. I've put in my order, and even if my Soulmate is on backorder, that's okay. I am living my best life and know that I will attract a man who is living his best life and is ready to work with me to create a beautiful life together.

I have learned so much, and even with all the bumps in the road, the journey has been educational. I have had the chance to take down the wall that was around my heart because I had always been so afraid of being hurt. I have learned to love myself first so that I would know how to love my next partner. I have learned that a woman is beautiful when she is standing in her truth and loves the skin she is in.

The radiance that shines through your eyes when you are happy is incredible. No man can resist the beauty of authenticity. You are enough, and you are amazingly beautiful. Shine in your beauty. You will attract the perfect man for you when you are clear about who you are.

Live in the space of gratitude. Give to others those things that you desire. Love your family and friends openly and authentically. Create the life you are passionate about. Give yourself a chance to really know who you are, and then go out and have some fun online.

Thank you for going on this journey with me. I hope you have enjoyed reading this book as much as I've enjoyed writing it. I hope I have opened a door that has allowed you to laugh and learn and love. Never give up on yourself because you deserve the very best.

Chapter 41

THE TAKE-AWAYS

When I set out to document my online journey, I had no idea how much I would learn and how much I would want to share to help other women avoid the mistakes I made and develop an educated, and more comfortable approach to online dating. I have offered tips, tricks, and aha moments to give you a glimpse into the online world, granted from my perspective, but hopefully to offer you a relaxed perspective.

I would be remiss if I didn't offer an easy-to-access guide to some of the most salient ideas. Here's a list of things I think you should know.

Spotting Imposters

There are some patterns that I have noticed the scammers use. If you respond to their flirt, they will immediately come back with an extremely long letter documenting who they are, how long they have been widowed, and how beautiful you are. The letter comes too soon and is far to "pre-programmed" to be a spontaneous reply.

Read their texts carefully! Is their English a little off? Do they put a space after the punctuation at the end of each sentence? Those educated in other countries do not follow the same spacing rules we follow in the U.S.

I have mentioned this in the book, but it's worth repeating it here, as well. There is a story that seems to be far, too, familiar. His wife died six years ago either from cancer or in a car accident on the way home from work. She was either a nurse or a teacher. There is one child who is going to school in Europe. For work, he is either a Construction Engineer or a Gemologist! He is ready to retire after he finishes this last huge contract (he will send you a "picture" of it so you know it's true.) He is going out of the country to build a huge structure as part of a government contract, or he is traveling to South Africa to buy precious gems and diamonds!

He will woo you day after day with his notes getting more passionate as time goes by. He misses you and can't wait to get back home to retire and make a new life with you.

…And then, oh no! He is overseas, his machinery breaks down, his credit card won't work, and won't you send him $29,000?! Block him! Unmatch him! Do whatever it takes to have no further conversations with him. Don't ever send money….not a dime!

Hopefully you haven't given him your address, phone number or email. Just break free and know it was a lesson worth learning.

Another common scam to watch out for is you will get a note saying:

I am sorry to intrude, but I promised to write to you. I have found the woman of my dreams on this website, but I was trying to encourage my cousin to try online dating, so we were looking at profiles and when we came across yours, he was so interested. He asked me to write to you to see if you would write to him.

He is a wonderful guy, tall and handsome. He is in your age group and lives near you. You have nothing to lose. Please take a chance and email him at blabla@anysite.com. You will be glad you did.

Once again, block the account and do not email the other person. It's a scam.

Protecting Yourself

Since we are talking about protecting yourself, there are a few things you can do. Sign up for a Google phone number. It's free and your message is on 24 hours a day. When someone leaves you a message, you will get an email and both the recorded message and the transcription of the message. You will be able to hear his voice and choose whether or not to reply.

You can also create an anonymous email account. When you create it, use a fictitious name? I think it's better to have these in place for when you want to talk offline, but don't yet feel comfortable with him. I actually tell the man that I always protect my personal information and I am happy to give him my fictitious email so that we can correspond. You don't need to lie, but you also don't need to reveal too much in the beginning.

Background Checks

Do those words conjure up fear and trepidation in you? Don't worry, it is just another way to protect yourself. There are some simple things you can do. Google his name. Do a Facebook search of his name. Pay the fee and look him up with a complete report from Spokeo. Take his photo and do a Google image search. If he has given you his phone number, do a Whitepages search.

Dating Sites

I have some favorite sites:

eHarmony is a subscription site. It costs money and takes a long time to answer all the questions so that your psychological profile can be created from your answers.

Elite Singles and Silver Singles. I put them together because the database of names is shared between them. They are both costly sites, but you will find more educated people there. They also do a personality assessment so you can see traits such as emotional stability, extroversion, introversion, agreeableness, and others. I have found the largest number of compatible men there.

Match offers the least amount of information about the men in the database. It does not have a great number of well-educated people, so if that's what you are looking for, perhaps you should check out one of the others. You can use a Match Boost which promotes your profile for an hour for an additional fee. They also offer you the chance to talk with a dating expert.

Big Beautiful People Meet. This is a site for people who are overweight or for those who are attracted to the overweight. It seems to attract more people who are more interested in a physical relationship than anything else.

Ok Cupid I haven't gotten a sense of this being a website that attracts one type of person over another. I have corresponded with a variety of men from those who are educated to those who are not. OKCupid offers lots of questions to answer and you are matched with someone who has answered with the highest percent of similar answers.

Italian People Meet (or Christian People Meet or you can pretty much fill in the blanks.) The databases are similar though if you pay for one, you don't get access to the others. They offer you suggested partners.

Most of the sites offer you the chance to see who has looked at your profile, who has sent you a flirt and who has written you a message.

Sex

No judgment here, but if you are strictly looking for a hookup, there are sites like Tinder for that. If, however, you are looking for a total relationship, I would avoid hook up sites. You will be sending the wrong message if you are on those sites.

In the Journal of Sex Research, it states that men think about sex nineteen times an hour and women think about sex ten times an hour. That means that men think about sex twice as often as women. Ladies, don't be naïve! Before you venture into online dating, you need to think about your values and your needs.

There should be no surprises when you go out with someone that he will bring up the subject of when you will be comfortable enough to get intimate with him. He's thinking about it all the time, so you had better think about how you feel before he broaches the subject.

We live in the 21st century, you need to protect yourself against sexually transmitted diseases, so get tested and insist he get tested too before you go down that road. If you aren't ready to have that conversation, you really aren't ready for online dating.

Your Profile

I am firmly convinced that the way you write your profile makes all the difference in the world. Talk about all aspects of your life, but don't reveal any personal information. If you are lucky enough to be financially secure, don't talk about it…scammers home in on that! You can talk about the importance of family, your hobbies, your desire for a complete relationship, etc. There are both men and women who put so little in their profile that no one can figure out who they are or what they stand for. Those people get passed by all the time. If you are serious about hearing from someone, take time and write a good profile. If writing about yourself is hard, ask a friend to give you some adjectives that describe who you are and use that information to write your profile. It should really represent who you are.

The Good Guys

I worry that in my quest to inform and protect you, I may have missed the most important thing of all…the good guys! There are amazing and wonderfully real men out there who will love and protect you. If you are looking for your Soulmate, you will find him. Just as you are real and sincere, there are men online who are as sincere as you are.

Take some time to think about those qualities in a man that you love and need and those that are deal breakers. Once you know what you want, call in your Soulmate. Concentrate on that man who is perfect for you. He will come in when you least expect it, and you will love every minute of your new relationship. Be open, be honest, and embrace the experience.

I wish you luck. I wish you love. I wish you lasting happiness forever!

Additional Resources

National Sexual Violence Resource Center
1-877-739-3895 | www.nsvrc.org

Rape, Abuse, and Incest National Network (RAINN)
Hotline 1-800-656-HOPE (4673) | www.rainn.org

National Domestic Violence Hotline
1-800-799-SAFE (7233) or 1-800-787-3224 | www.thehotline.org

Planned Parenthood
1-800-230-7526 | www.plannedparenthood.org

Cyber Civil Rights Initiative
1-844-878-2274 | www.cybercivilrights.org

FBI Internet Crime Complaint Center www.ic3.gov

National Human Trafficking Hotline
1-888-373-7888 or text 233733 | www.humantraffickinghotline.org

National Center for Missing & Exploited Children
1-800-THE-LOST (843-5678) | www.cybertipline.com

Chapter 42

JOIN ME

D o you have an online dating story you would love to share with the world? In my next book on online dating, I want to give you the opportunity to join me on an adventure. Share your stories with me so that I can include them in the book. Please change all of the names so as not to offend anyone, but tell the truth, and tell us the lessons you have learned. We are all sisters, and as such, we need to stick together to help each other grow and flourish, learn what to avoid and recognize the aha moments. If you have a wonderful dating story to tell, please send it to _Boomerchickdating@gmail.com_. I look forward to all you share. I thank you in advance for joining me in my quest to help other boomer chicks find love in a safe and positive way. Share the lessons you've learned and share your joy because we are never too old to look and love!

ABOUT ANGELA

Angela I. Schutz, M.A.

Angela I. Schutz is the Managing Director and Founder of Driven To Succeed Consulting LLC, a career development and executive coaching service aimed at empowering people to find their ultimate career potential. She has also served as a University Relations Career Consultant and a Certified Associate for Lee Hecht Harrison, an international career management organization ranked second in outplacement services. Ms. Schutz served as a career consultant to hundreds of clients and to students earning their MBA and EMBA degrees.

Ms. Schutz has served as the Executive Director of Training and Development for the National Society of Leadership and Success. In this capacity her duties included serving as the online success coach for undergraduate students across the country who were members of this national honor society. She also served as the primary support person for chapter advisors and student chapter presidents. Her duties extended to areas of sales, marketing, and publicity.

Ms. Schutz received her academic education at Gateway Community College where she earned her Associates Degree and Southern Connecticut State University where she earned her Bachelor of Arts in Psychology. She completed her graduate work at the University of New Haven where she earned a Master of Arts in Community Psychology.

Ms. Schutz exhibits a true love of learning and strives to mentor students through her professional passion. She is a qualified Myers-Briggs Type Indicator Administrator and holds a Management Certificate in Higher Education from the Higher Education Resource Service (HERS) from Wellesley College.

In 2009, Ms. Schutz was chosen as one of 100 individuals from around the world to take part in the Train the Trainer program with author Jack Canfield. She is certified to teach success empowerment workshops. She is a professional speaker and speaks on topics that span all phases of career development as well as success empowerment. She holds five Career Consultation certifications. She has facilitated career learning sessions for such organizations as Women for Hire.

She is a certified Dream Coach through Dream Coach University® founded by Marcia Wieder and has studied Neuro-Linguistic Programming with Sean Smith.

She is a Senior Career Coach for Career Curve, an outplacement organization in Cleveland, Ohio. She is also an adjunct professor at Gateway Community College. She is committed to the education of college students and has established a scholarship for that purpose at Gateway Community College. She resides in Connecticut and is a proud mother and grandmother.

In 2020-2021, she was inducted into Who's Who in America and in 2021-2022 she was inducted into Who's Who in Professional Women. She is truly honored and humbled by these awards.

She is an accomplished author. She wrote, Career Questions? Ask Angela - A Job-Seeker's Guide to Finding the Perfect Job. She has been published in eight books on gratitude, a book on pets, on independence, in a women's anthology and **The Book on Joy.** **A Boomer Chick's Guide to Online Dating** is her second book.

For more infomation about Angela I. Schutz please visit www.Boomer-Chick.com and www.driventosucceed.net

CPSIA information can be obtained
at www.ICGtesting.com
Printed in the USA
BVHW051420061221
623332BV00012B/275